1,000,000 Books

are available to read at

www.ForgottenBooks.com

Read online
Download PDF
Purchase in print

ISBN 978-1-332-93969-5
PIBN 10440517

1 MONTH OF
FREE
READING

at

www.ForgottenBooks.com

By purchasing this book you are eligible for one month membership to ForgottenBooks.com, giving you unlimited access to our entire collection of over 1,000,000 titles via our web site and mobile apps.

To claim your free month visit:

www.forgottenbooks.com/free440517

A TREASURY OF CATHOLIC SONG

COMPRISING SOME TWO HUNDRED HYMNS
FROM CATHOLIC SOURCES OLD AND NEW

GATHERED, EDITED
AND ALLOTTED TO FITTING TUNES
FOR CONGREGATIONAL USE

BY

SIDNEY S. HURLBUT

PASTOR OF ST. MARY'S CHURCH, HAGERSTOWN, MARYLAND

' Sanguis Christi, inebria me ut cum sanctis Tuis laudem Te in saecula saeculorum. Amen."

FOR THE EDITOR
J. FISCHER & BRO., PUBLISHERS
NEW YORK CITY
1915

Imprimatur

James Card. Gibbons

Archbishop of Baltimore

Baltimore, February, 1915

Approved

James N. McGean

Chairman, Diocesan Church Music Commission

New York, March, 1915

Imprimatur

Remigius Lafort S.T.D.

Librorum Censor

Peekskill, N. Y., March, 1915

To those I have known and loved
Who share the bliss of God's elect
And delight in His comely praise

PREFACE

The collection of Hymns and Tunes here put forth has been designed primarily for the Editor's own Parish. It is witness to a conviction that sacred song s not only a natural and fitting vehicle of Christian devotion, but its reflex value is great, in that genuine, wholesome, virile religious spirit may be powerfully fostered and stimulated by worthy Christian song. Endeavor is here made to present, in ample variety, hymnic matter for processional and recessional use, as well as for non-liturgical services in Church, for Low Mass, Benediction, Way of the Cross, Devotions for Lent, to the Holy Eucharist, to the Sacred Heart, the Holy Name, the Blessed Virgin Mary; and to uphold consistently, for the Glory of God and the spread of His Kingdom, a two-fold standard of excellence, Good Verse and Good Music: Verse not more correct doctrinally than suitable for devotional use by Catholic congregations, while conformed to the canons of literary shape and rhythmic flow; Music not lacking in expression of the varying phases of prayer and praise, yet marked throughout by a certain "nobility of form" befitting sacred use and in keeping with the *notu proprio* "code" of the lamented Pope Pius X. With what success others must judge; but to search out and bring together only the excellent, with due regard to availability in our day and the exigencies of times and seasons, not sparing cost and regardless of whatever personal predilection or tender association, such has been through long labor of love the Editor's unvarying aim. Idea of compromise to satisfy divergent and drooping taste has not for a moment been entertained.

Catholic sources alone have been drawn on for words of this collection. From first to last every hymn presented is of undoubted Catholic authorship. The greater number of them were written in the traditional Latin of the Church and have been hallowed by centuries of pious use in the household of the faith: of these, in spirit of highest honor for the originals, preference is given to such translations, by whomsoever made, as in the Editor's view seem to combine, in best measure, fidelity to writer's thought, happy English diction and itness to musical setting. The latter quality oftentimes suffices to turn the scale, and in a few cases the problem of choice among translations has found solution in a cento.

The fact that many of our Catholic hymns, both original and translated, were written with no distinct view to musical use, entails frequent employment of the "editorial file" if one will do away with halting metres, than which some think a more glaring fault can scarcely disfigure a hymn-book. When possible an Author has been consulted as to minor changes in his text, but in many more cases consultation has been impossible, the Author's glad approval has been presumed, and his work thus gently fitted to fluent Christian song. Is this to mutilate or destroy? No, it is to establish. Disrespect to a writer, will some say? Rightly viewed, rather is it not to honor him the more?

Tunes in this book, taken *en masse,* are likewise from Composers who have gloried in Catholic name. Ages past and the fleeting twentieth century, Continental Europe, Britain, Ireland, America, all have furnished their quota of loyal enlistment. Many tunes of great merit by Catholic Composers, that among our people are quite unknown or well-nigh completely forgotten, it is a special pleasure to include and as from alien grasp reclaim. Benefit of doubt moreover is taken with certain fine old tunes of which the Composer's identity and status can not be learned, while only for the exactions of peculiar metre is a modicum of original melody admitted. Finally, if in few instances musical work known to be of other than Catholics be found herein, the marked excellence and devotional value of the tunes is thought to afford warrant in Christian charity for their use, especially since in no case are they coupled with words of non-catholic vogue. Tunes ascribed to non-catholic Composers are about sixteen in number: their inclusion here is subject to correction: if authority or sound criticism so bid, they may be omitted from future editions of this work.

After saints and heroes of God who long since or but yesterday entered into rest, whose songs yet re-echo here the good and the true, grateful acknowledgment of favors received is extended to the following:

Mr. Julius Bas, for Gregorian harmonies:
The Rev. Fr. John J. Burke, C.S.P., for tunes by the late Father Alfred Young:
The Rev. Dom Bede Camm, O.S.B., for a beautiful hymn to the Blessed Virgin Mary:
Messrs. Cary & Co., London, for several fine tunes by Sir Edward Elgar and others:
The Rt. Rev. L. C. Casartelli, D.D., Bishop of Salford, for a translation in honor of St Joseph:
The Rev. Fr. F. C. Devas, S.J., for his happy lines to St. Ignatius:

The Hon. D. J. Donahoe, may whose muse long enthral us, for generous permission to draw from his two volumes of beautifully translated "Early Chrisian Hymns":

Messrs. J. Fischer & Bro., for many tunes collected by the late Dr. A. E. Tozer nd covered by their copyright:

Mr. Charles T. Gatty, for share in the wealth of exquisite music stored in his monumental work for English Catholics, "Arundel Hymns":

The Rev. Dr. H. T. Henry, for kind permission to use his lines in centonization nd for superb translations taken from his "Eucharistica":

Messrs. Novello & Co., London, for a tune by Charles Gounod:

The Rev. Fr. John O'Connor, for translations and original verse of rarest eauty:

The Rev. Dom S. Gregory Ould, O.S.B., for selections from his "Book of Iymns":

The house of L. Schwann, Duesseldorf, for a fine tune by Joseph Groiss:

Mr. Orby Shipley, who through his "Annus Sanctus" and "Carmina Mariana" as made all English-reading Catholics his debtors:

Dr. R. R. Terry, editor of the "Westminster Hymnal," for excellent tunes and rrangements:

The French Vincentian Fathers, for several selections from their "Cantuale":

Mr. Wilfrid Ward, for verses of Aubrey de Vere:

Mr. George Herbert Wells, for a tune, for harmonizations, musical arrange-nents and proof-reading; his patient collaboration and ready counsel have been imply invaluable at every stage of the Editor's task:

The Rev. Fr. J. B Young, S.J., for helpful suggestions and for harmonies ound in his "Roman Hymnal."

Diligent effort has been made to communicate with Authors, Composers and ith owners of copyrights. If any rights have been unwittingly infringed, apology hereby offered with promise of due reparation. Original work herein, musical nd literary, likewise revisions, arrangements and adaptations, are covered by the ditor's copyright.

While it is foreseen that many will hastily disregard this collection as unprac-cal, unsympathetic, uncalled for or what not, one ventures the thought *"Qui otest capere, capiat."* As time passes and the Papal Reform of Liturgical Music ains more general appreciation and wider sway, those interested will judge hether, in the minor sphere of Hymnody, some measure of encouragement and source, contributive to the beauty of divine worship and to intelligent devotion. ay possibly be derived from this little Treasury of Catholic Song.

St. Mary's,
Hagerstown, Maryland,
Feast of the Purification, 1915.

CONTENTS CLASSIFIED

A Treasury of Catholic Song

MORNING

Aurora jam spargit polum

1 Mor - ning shines with Eas - tern Light; Earth is glad the
2 So, when breaks our la - test morn, And we rise our
3 Glo - ry to the Fa - ther be, E - qual glo - ry

day to see; Flee, ye phan - toms of the night;
Lord to meet, Songs shall wel - come in its dawn,
to the Son, With the Spi - rit, One and Three,

Thoughts and deeds of dark - ness, flee.
Shouts of joy its com - ing greet. A - men.
While e - ter - nal a - ges run:

MORNING
Splendor paternae gloriae

1. Splen - dor of the Fa - ther's Glo - ry,
2. Tru - est Sun, up - on us brigh - ten
3. Christ, be Thou our Bread from Hea - ven

Source of all things fair to sight, Light of Light, let
With Thy pure and con - stant gleam; Fill our hearts, our
And our cup, faith's ho - ly light, Whence the Spi - rit,

all a - dore Thee, Day in Whom the day is bright.
spi - rits ligh - ten, With Thy Spi - rit's clean-sing stream. A-men.
free - ly giv - en, Shall with us Him - self u - nite.

4. So our day, serenely flowing,
  Pure will be as morning dawn;
  Bright our faith like noontide glowing,
  O'er our eye no darkness drawn.

5. Now all praise and adoration
  To the Blessed Trinity;
  Praise our God through time's duration;
  Praise Him through eternity.

MORNING
Aeterna coeli gloria

1. Christ, the Glo - ry of the sky, Christ, of earth the
2. Help us now Thy praise to sing, Praise for this re -
3. Pu - rest Light, with - in us dwell, Nev - er from our

hope se - cure, On - ly Son of God most high,
tur - ning day; Light and life let mor - ning bring,
souls de - part; Come, the shades of earth ex - pel,

Off - spring of the Mai - den pure.
Clouds and dark - ness flee a - way. A - men
Fill and pu - ri - fy the heart.

4. Faith in Him Whose Name we bear,
In our heart of hearts abound;
Hope, thy brightest torch prepare;
All with holy Love be crowned.

5. Praise the Father; praise the Son;
Spirit blest, to Thee be praise;
To th' eternal Three in One
Glory be through endless days.

MORNING
Nox et tenebrae et nubila

1. Swift as sha - dows of the night
2. To Thy light, O heaven - ly King,
3. Ma - ny stains our souls de - file;

Haste be - fore the mor - ning light,
Un - di - vi - ded hearts we bring,
Ma - ny snares to sin be - guile;

Powers of dark - ness quick - ly fly;
Seek in praise and prayer Thy grace,
Much we need Thy light di - vine;

See the Day - spring from on high.
Hide not, Lord, from us Thy face. A - men.
Light of An - gels, on us shine.

4. Glory be to God on high;
Father, Thee we magnify,
Equally the Son adore,
And the Spirit evermore.

MORNING
Lux ecce surgit aurea

1. As at morn's gol - den ray Flee the sha - dows of
2. To Thine all - see - ing eye Eve - ry se - cret is
3. Let our thoughts then be clean And our ac - tions be

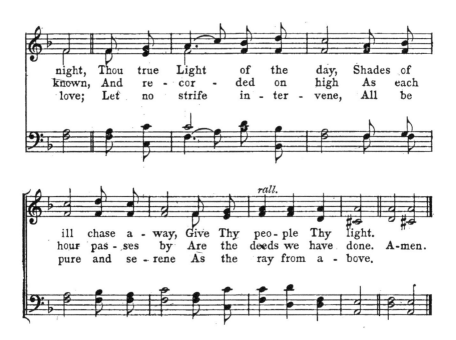

night, Thou true Light of the day, Shades of
known, And re - cor - ded on high As each
love; Let no strife in - ter - vene, All be

ill chase a - way, Give Thy peo - ple Thy light.
hour pas - ses by Are the deeds we have done. A - men.
pure and se - rene As the ray from a - bove.

4. To the Father be praise,
Equal praise to the Son
And the Spirit always,
While the infinite days
Of eternity run.

MORNING
Rector potens verax Deus

1. Thou Who canst nev - er change nor fail,
2. Quench Thou the fires of hate and strife,
3. Grant this, O Fa - ther, on - ly Son

Gui - ding the hours as they roll by,
The wa - sting fe - ver of the heart;
And Ho - ly Spi - rit, God of grace,

Brighte - ning with beams the mor - ning pale And
From per - ils guard our fee - ble life And
To Whom all glo - ry, Three in One, Be

glow - ing warm in mid - day sky.
to our souls Thy peace im - part. A - men.
given in eve - ry time and place.

Conditor alme siderum

1. Cre - a - tor of the star - ry skies, Thy
2. When man was sunk in sin and death, When
3. Thou, for the sake of guil - ty men, Per -

peo-ple's Light for ev - er-more, Je - sus, Re - dee - mer
lost in depth of Sa - tan's snare, Love brought Thee down to
mit - ting Thy pure Blood to flow, Didst is - sue from Thy

of man-kind, Be near us who Thine aid im-plore.
cure our ills By ta-king of those ills a share. A-men.
Vir-gin shrine And to the Cross a Vic-tim go.

4. So great the glory of Thy might,
   If we but chance Thy Name to sound,
   At once all Heaven and hell unite
   In bending low with awe profound.

5. Great Judge of all, in that last day,
   When friends shall fail and foes combine,
   Be present then with us we pray
   To guard us with Thine arm divine.

6. To God the Father, with the Son
   And Holy Spirit, One in Three,
   Be honor, glory, blessing, praise,
   All through the long eternity.

8

ADVENT

Verbum supernum prodiens

1. Su - per - nal Word, pro - cee - ding from Th'E -
2. En - ligh - ten, Lord, and set on fire Our
3. So when be - fore the judg - ment - seat The

ter - nal Fa - ther's breast, And
spi - rits with Thy love, That
sin - ner hears his doom, And

in the course of a - ges come To
dead to earth we may as - pire And
when a voice di - vine - ly sweet Shall

aid a world dis - tressed: A - men.
live to joys a - bove:
call the righ - teous home,

Tune from Arundel Hymns by permission.

4. Safe from the black and fiery flood,
   That sweeps the dread abyss,
   We may behold the face of God
   In everlasting bliss.

5. To God the Father, with the Son
   And Spirit, evermore
   Be glory while the ages run,
   As in all time before.

Instantis adventum Dei

1. The Com - ing of our God Must now our thoughts em -
2. The co - e - ter - nal Son A Mai - den's Off - spring
3. In glo - ry from His throne A - gain will Christ de -

ploy; Then let us meet Him . on the road With
see; A ser - vant's form Christ put - teth on To
scend, And sum - mon all that are His own To

songs of ho - ly joy.
make His peo - ple free. A - men.
joys that nev - er end.

4. Let deeds of darkness fly
Before th' approaching morn,
For unto sin 'tis ours to die,
And serve the Virgin - born.

5. Our joyful praises sing
To Christ that set us free,
Like tribute to the Father bring,
And Holy Ghost to Thee.

ADVENT
En clara vox redarguit

1. Hark, a Her - ald Voice is call - ing;
2. Star - tled at the sol - emn war - ning,
3. Now the Lamb so long ex - pec - ted

'Christ is nigh,' it seems to say; 'Cast a - way the
Let the earth-bound soul a - rise; Christ, her Sun, all
Comes with par - don down from Heaven; Let us haste, with

dreams of dark - ness, O ye - chil-dren of the Day.'
sloth dis - pel - ling, Shines up - on the mor-ning skies. A-men.
tears of sor - row, One and all to be for - given.

Tune from Catholic Church Hymnal by permission of J. Fischer & Bro.

4. So, when next He comes with glory,
Wrapping all the earth in fear,
May He then as our Defender
On the clouds of heaven appear.

5. Honor, glory, virtue, merit,
To the Father and the Son,
With the co-eternal Spirit,
While unending ages run.

Tandem fluctus tandem luctus

1. Storm and ter - ror, grief and er - ror,
2. O true Splen - dor, bright and ten - der,
3. Now Thou kee - pest rest and slee - pest

Comes the Sun to chase a - way, And the mor - ning,
Sun of Righ - teous - ness on high, Port Thou show - est,
In that zo - diac of de - light, Joy here - af - ter

fast a - dor - ning All the sky, pro - claims the Day.
source Thou ow - est To the Vir - gin's pu - ri - ty. A-men.
shall with laugh - ter Hail the com - ing Mon - arch's sight.

From Catholic Church Hymnal by permission of J. Fischer & Bro.

4. Satan gnashing sees it flashing
   Through that cloud so pure and white,
   Thou endurest ever purest,
   Virgin Mother of the Light.

5. Earth rejoices, heavenly voices
   Render praise to God above,
   Now renewing and bedewing
   Every soul with fuller love.

ADVENT

Veni, veni Emmanuel

1. O come, O come, Em - ma - nu - el,
2. O come, Thou Rod of Jes - se, free
3. O come, Thou Day - spring, come and cheer

And ran - som cap - tive Is - ra - el,
Thine own from Sa - tan's ty - ran - ny;
Our spi - rits by Thine Ad - vent here;

That mourns in lone - ly ex - ile here
From depths of hell Thy peo - ple save
Dis - perse the gloo - my clouds of night

Un - til the Son of God ap - pear.
And give them vic - tory o'er the grave.
And earth's dark sha - dows put to flight.

Re - joice! Re - joice! Em ma - nu - el
Re - joice! Re - joice! Em ma - nu - el
Re - joice! Re - joice! Em ma - nu - el

Shall come to thee O Is - ra - el.
Shall come to thee O Is - ra - el. A - men.
Shall come to thee O Is - ra - el.

4. O come, Thou Key of David, come
And open wide our Heavenly Home;
Make safe the way that leads on high
And close the path to misery.
Rejoice!........

5. O come, O come, Thou Lord of Might,
Who to Thy tribes on Sinai's hight
In ancient times didst give the law
In cloud and majesty and awe.
Rejoice!........

1. All the skies to - night sing o'er us.
2. Glo - ry in the high - est Hea - ven
3. Sons of men, let no - thing grieve you.

Sweet and far Star to star Ma - keth sol - emn cho - rus.
And a - gain Un - to men Tru - est Peace be giv - en.
Ev - er-more Hea - ven's door Wi - dens to re - ceive you.

Time the mid - night blest is tel - ling When our Lord
All our wrong by Him is righ - ted In Whose Birth
Bro - thers of the Babe E - ter - nal, In His Name

God the Word Made with us His dwel - ling.
Heaven and earth Stand for ay u - ni - ted. A - men.
Come and claim Grace and bliss su - per - nal.

From Arundel Hymns by permission.

CHRISTMAS

Jesu Redemptor omnium

1. O per - fect Noon of Love - li - ness, A -
2. Thy - self His un - be - gin - ning Ray, So
3. O Thou Who all things fair dost plan, Re -

blaze ere an - y mor-ning woke! O Je - sus, Thee the
Thou art our un - en - ding cheer: Bend low as earth a
mem - ber how the Mo - ther mild Her sub-stance gave Thee,

Fa - ther spoke, Com - peer of all His peer-less-ness.
gra - cious ear To what Thy ser-vants ask to - day. A-men.
un - de - filed, And made Thee more than kin to man.

From Arundel Hymns by permission.

4. Bright witness is this day, the best
Of all the year's bejeweled crown,
That our distress beguiled Thee down,
O love-lorn God, from glorious rest.

5. Now earth and stars and heaving sea,
And all that heavenly influence own,
Their new-discovered praise intone,
O Fount of endless hope, to Thee.

6. And we, all gemmed with ruby rain
Outpouring from Thy love and life,
With all Thy creatures make sweet strife
To pay Thy Birth a seemly strain.

7. Of all Thy fair delights the most,
That Thou O Christ art Mary's Son,
Be this to Thee, Who still art One
With Sire Supreme and Holy Ghost

CHRISTMAS
A solis ortus cardine

1. From where the ri - sing sun as - cends To
2. The great Cre - a - tor deigns as - sume Our
3. By Heaven o'er - sha - dowed, filled with grace, A

where his dai - ly path-way ends, Through ev - 'ry re - gion
ser - vile form from Ma - ry's womb, That clothed in flesh He,
spot - less Maid of Da - vid's race, Sur - pas - sing na - ture's

let us sing The Mai - den's Offspring, Christ our King.
may re-claim The fal - len flesh Him - self did frame. A - men.
law, contains The fruit with-out the mo - ther's pains.

4. O dwelling ever pure and bright,
The fane where dwells the God of Might,
To which descends at Heaven's behest
The Word conceived in Mary's breast.

5. The Angel's voice the deed foretells,
And Christ within her bosom dwells,
And John unborn exults to find
The Lord made Flesh to save mankind.

6. In manger laid your Lord behold,
The hay His bed in winter's cold;
Behold Him fed on infant fare
Who feeds the feathered fowls of air.

7. And hark, the Choir Angelic raise
To God the joyful song of praise,
And bid the lowly shepherds know
The Shepherd-Lord of all below.

8. To God the Father, God the Son
Of Mary born, be homage done;
The like to God the Spirit be,
Eternal Godhead, One in Three.

Laetabundus exultet

1. Ye choirs of faith, re - joice and sing,
2. Dis - dai - ning not the Vir - gin's womb,
3. Of Ma - ry, shi - ning Star of Morn,

Your wreaths of love and prai - ses bring:
The An - gel of the Coun - cil come
The glo - rious Sun of Noon is born:

From stain - less Maid is born our King.
To earth from His Ce - les - tial Home.
With hymns and prayers His path a - dorn.

Al - le - lu - ia!
Al - le - lu - ia! A - men.
Al - le - lu - ia!

4. That Sun shall never setting know, 5. And as the Star sends forth its light,
That Star shall ever brightly glow, Unsullied by that radiance bright,
Our light above, our hope below. So Mary brings the King of Might.
Alleluia! Alleluia!

1. A - de - ste fi - de - les, Lae - ti tri - um - phan-tes, Ve -
2. De - um de De - o, Lu - men de lu - mi - ne,
3. En gre - ge re - lic - to, Hu - mi - les ad cu - nas, Vo -

4. Stel-la du - ce Ma - gi, Chri-stum a - do - ran - tes,
5. Ae - ter - ni Pa - ren-tis Splen-do - rem ae - ter-num Ve -
6. Pro no - bis e - ge-num Et foe - no cu - ban-tem
7. Can - tet nunc I - o Cho - rus an - ge - lo - rum,
8. Er - go qui na - tus Di - e ho - di - er - na

ni - te, ve - ni - te in Beth - le - hem:
Ge - stant pu - el - lae vi - sce - ra:
ca - ti pa - sto - res ap - pro - pe - rant:

Au - rum, thus et myr - rham dant mu - ne - ra:
la - tum sub Car - ne vi - de - bi - mus,
Pi - is fo - ve - a - mus am - plex - i - bus.
Can - tet nunc au - la coe - le - sti - um,
Je - su ti - bi sit glo - ri - a,

Na - tum vi - de - te Re - gem an - ge - lo - rum: Ve -
De - um   ve - rum, Ge - ni - tum non fac - tum: Ve -
Et nos o - van - ti Gra - du fe - sti - ne - mus: Ve -

Je - su In - fan - ti Cor - da prae - be - a - mus. Ve -
De - um In - fan - tem Pan - nis in - vo - lu - tum. Ve -
Sic nos a - man - tem Quis non re - da - ma - ret? Ve -
Glo -   ri - a In ex - cel - sis De - o! Ve -
Pa - tris ae - ter - ni Ver - bum ca - ro fac - tum. Ve -

ni - te a - do - re - mus, Ve - ni - te a - do - re - mus, Ve -

us   Do - mi - m. A - men.

CHRISTMAS
Adeste fideles

1. Come all ye faith-ful, Joy-ful and tri-um-phant,
2. God of God, Light of Light,
3. See how the shep-herds, Summoned to His cra-dle,
4. Lo, star-led chief-tains, Ma-gi, Christ a-do-ring,
5. Splen-dor e-ter-nal Of th'E-ter-nal Fa-ther,
6. Child for us sin-ners, Poor and in the man-ger,
7. Sing, Choirs of An-gels, Sing in ex-ul-ta-tion.
8. Yea, Lord, we greet Thee Born this hap-py mor-ning:

Come ye, O come ye to Beth-le-hem.
Lo He dis-dains not the Vir-gin's womb:
Lea-ving their flocks, draw nigh with low-ly fear:

Of-fer Him in-cense, gold and myrrh:
Veiled un-der hu-man flesh to greet hu-man view,
Fain we em-brace Thee with awe and love.
Sing, all ye ci-ti-zens of Heaven a-bove,
Je-sus, to Thee be glo-ry given,

Come and be-hold Him Born the King of An - gels. O
Ve - ry God Be - got - ten not cre - a - ted: O
We too will thith - er Bend our joy - ful foot - steps. O

We to the Christ Child Bring our heart's ob - la - tions. O
In - fi - nite De - i - ty, Wrapped in In - fant's clo - thing, O
Who would not love Thee Lov - ing us so dear - ly? O
Glo - ry to God In the High - est! O
Word of the Fa - ther Now in Flesh ap - pea - ring. O

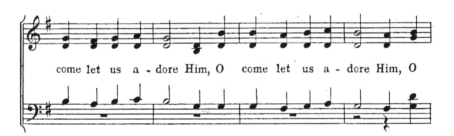

come let us a - dore Him, O come let us a - dore Him, O

come let us a - dore Him, Christ the Lord. A - men.

CHRISTMAS
Jure plaudant omnia

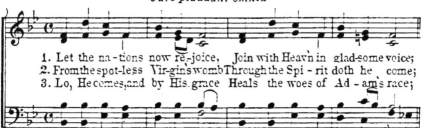

1. Let the na-tions now re-joice, Join with Heav'n in glad-some voice;
2. From the spot-less Vir-gin's womb Through the Spi-rit doth he come;
3. Lo, He comes, and by His grace Heals the woes of Ad-am's race;

Let the ti-dings of the morn Loud-ly ring, Loud-ly ring.
Peace and love for strife and scorn Doth He bring, Doth He bring.
Ri-sing from our lot for-lorn Let us sing, Let us sing.

Un-to us to-day is born Christ the King, Christ the King.
Un-to us to-day is born Christ the King, Christ the King. A-men.
For to us to-day is born Christ the King, Christ the King.

Tune from Westminster Hymnal.

4. Loving Jesus, evermore
   Thee we praise and Thee adore.
   Love to Thee both night and morn
   Shall we bring, Shall we bring:
   Unto us to-day is born
   Christ the King, Christ the King.

1. An - gels we have heard on high Sweet - ly sing - ing
2. Shep - herds, why this Ju - bi - lee? Why this ec - sta -
3. Come to Beth - l'em, come and see Him Whose Birth the

o'er the plains, And the moun-tains in re - ply Ech-o - ing their
sy of song? Say what may the ti-dings be That in-spire yon
An-gels sing: Come, a-dore on ben-ded knee Je-sus Christ the

joy - ous strains: Glo - - -
heaven-ly throng? Glo - - -
In - fant King. Glo - -

- ri - a in ex - cel - sis De - o.
- ri - a in ex - cel - sis De - o. A-men.
- ri - a in ex - cel - sis De - o.

4. See within a manger laid
Jesus, Lord of Heaven and earth:
Mary, Joseph, lend your aid
To acclaim our Saviour's Birth:
Gloria in excelsis Deo.

1. Stars of glo-ry, shine more brightly, Pu-rer be the moonlight's beam,
2. See a beauteous An-gel soa-ring In the bright ce-les-tial blaze;
3. See the shepherds quick-ly ri-sing, Hastening to the hum-ble stall,

Glide ye hours and mo-ments light-ly, Swift-ly down time's deepening stream:
On the shepherds, low a - do-ring, Rest his mild ef - ful-gent rays.
And the new-born In-fant pri-zing As the migh-ty Lord of all.

Bring the hour that ban - ished sadness, Brought re-demption down to earth,
'Fear not' cries the heaven-ly stran-ger; 'Him Whom ancient seers foretold,
Low-ly now they bend be - fore Him In His help-less in-fant state,

When the shepherds heard with gladness Ti-dings of a Sa-viour's Birth.
Wee-ping in a low - ly manger, Shepherds, haste ye to be - hold! Amen.
Firm-ly faith-ful, they a - dore Him And His greatness cel-e - brate.

4. Hark, the swell of heavenly voices
Peals along the vaulted sky;
Angels sing, while earth rejoices,
Glory to our God on high,
Glory in the highest Heaven,
Peace to humble men on earth;
Joy to these and bliss is given
In the great Redeemer's Birth!

Tune from   *Westminster Hymnal.*

Parvum quando cerno Deum

1. Oft as Thee, my Infant Saviour, In Thy
2. Happy Babe and happy Mother, O how
3. As the dawn from darkness springing Sheds a

Mother's arms I view, Straight a thousand thrilling
great your bliss must be, Each enfolded in the
charm o'er nature's face, So the Child to Mary

raptures Penetrate my heart anew.
other, Breathing pure felicity. Amen.
clinging Decks her with diviner grace.

From Catholic Church Hymnal by permission of J. Fischer & Bro.

4. Lovely Jesus, gentle Brother,
   How I wish a smile from Thee,
   Meant for Thy immortal Mother,
   Only might alight on me.

CHRISTMAS

Corde natus ex parentis

1. Of the Fa - ther's love be - got - ten
2. At His word the worlds were fra - med:
3. He is found in hu - man fash - ion,

Ere the worlds be - gan to be,
He com - man - ded; it was done:
Death and sor - row here to know,

He is Al - pha and O - me - ga,
Heaven and earth and depths of o - cean
That the race of Ad - am's chil - dren

He the source, the en - ding He,
In their three - fold or - der one;
Doomed by law to end - less woe,

Of	the	things	that	are,	that	have	been,
All	that	grows	be -	neath	the	shi -	ning
May	not	hence -	forth	die	and	per -	ish

that	fu -		ars	shall	s(
the	moon		ir -	ning	s'
the	dread		ilf	be -	l(

Ev -	er -	more	and	ev -	er -	more.	
Ev -	er -	more	and	ev -	er -	more.	A - men.
Ev -	er -	more	and	ev -	er -	more.	

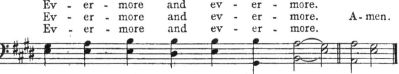

) that Birth for ever blessed,
Vhen the Virgin full of grace,
3y the Holy Ghost conceiving,
3ore the Saviour of our race,
\nd the Babe, the world's Redeemer,
°irst revealed His sacred face,
ivermore and evermore.

'his is He Whom seers in old time
'hanted of with one accord,
Vhom the voices of the prophets
'romised in their faithful word:
Vow He shines, the long-expected.
et creation praise its Lord
ivermore and evermore.

6. O ye Hights of Heaven adore Him;
   Angel - Hosts His praises sing;
   All Dominions bow before Him
   And extol our God and King.
   Let no tongue on earth be silent,
   Every voice in concert ring,
   Evermore and evermore.

7. Thee let old men, Thee let young men,
   Thee let boys in chorus sing;
   Matrons, virgins, little maidens,
   Glad their voices answering;
   Let their guileless songs re-echo
   And the heart its praises bring
   Evermore and evermore.

8. Christ, to Thee, with God the Father,
   And O Holy Ghost to Thee,
   Hymn and chant, with all thanksgiving
   And unwearied pra ses be,
   Honor, glory and dominion,
   And eternal victory,
   Evermore and evermore.

CHRISTMAS
Gloria in altissimis Deo

O Chris - tian, a - rise, and with

ca - rols Of grate - ful and ju - bi - lant

song, Re - soun - ding from earth to the

Fine.

wel - kin, The mes - sage of Christ - mas pro - long.

1. Of Ma - r . Vir - gin re - mem - ber, That
2. By far t st beau - teous of chil - dren, Di -
3. How pre - ci at hea - ven - ly mes - sage To

id - night in Beth - le - hem's stall,
ne how - e'er hum - ble His Birth,
ep - herds on Ju - de - an hill,

Was born the A - wai - ted of Na - tions, The
What love must it be that im - pelled Him For
All Glo - ry to God in the High - est And

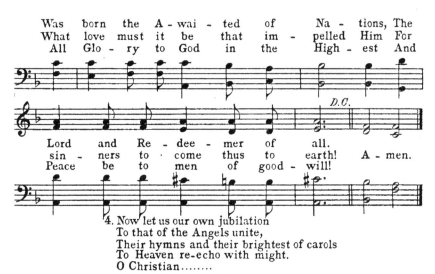

Lord and Re - dee - mer of all.
sin - ners to come thus to earth! A - men.
Peace be to men of good - will!

4. Now let us our own jubilation
   To that of the Angels unite,
   Their hymns and their brightest of carols
   To Heaven re-echo with might.
   O Christian........

5. The manger where Mary laid Jesus
   Surrounding, with tenderest love,
   Let praise and devotion most grateful
   Ascend to Him reigning above.
   O Christian........

CHRISTMASTIDE

Quem pastores laudavere

1. Shep-herds, tell your beau-teous sto - ry, How the daz - zling
2. Beth - le - hem hath now be - hol-den Kings of tribes far -
3. So with Ma - ry's glad-ness blen-ding, Let our thank-ful-

An - gel - glo - ry Sang to Ju - da's hill-sides hoa - ry
off and ol - den, In - cense, myrrh, and trea-sure gol - den,
ness, as - cen - ding, Scale high Heaven in sweet con - ten - ding

'Born is your E - ter - nal King.' A - men.
To her conque-ring Li - on bring.
With the An - gels' glo - rious choir.

From Arundel Hymns by permission.

4. God with us through Mary dwelleth;
   This dear grace all praise excelleth;
   Let the song such bliss that telleth
   In its own great joy expire.

1. The Lord and King of all things But yes-ter-day was born,
2. Come ye that love the Mar - tyrs, And pluck the flowers of song,
3. Thou first of all Con - fes - sors, Of all the Dea-cons crown,

And Ste-phen's glo-rious offe - ring His birth-tide shall a - dorn.
And weave them in a gar - land For this our sup-pliant throng,
Of eve - ry follo-wing ath - lete The glo - ry and re - nown,

No pearls of o-rient splen-dor, No jew - els can he show,
And cry 'O thou that shi - nest In gra - ce's brigh-test ray,
Make sup - pli - ca - tion, stan-ding Be - fore the King en - throned,

But with his own true heart's blood His shi - ning vestments glow.
Christ's val-iant Pro-to-mar - tyr, For peace and fa - vor pray. Amen.
That we may see His beau - ty Who for our sins a - toned.

1. Saint of the Sa - cred Heart, Sweet Tea - cher
2. Thou to whom grace was given To stand where
3. When the last eve - ning came, Thy head was

of the Word, Part - ner of Ma - ry's woes,
Pe - ter fell, Whose heart could brook the Cross
on His breast, Pil - lowed on earth where now

And favo - rite of the Lord:
Of Him it loved so well: A - men.
In Heaven the Saints find rest.

Tune from Arundel Hymns by permission.

4. His Heart with quickened love,
   Knowing His hour drew near,
   Now throbbed against thy head,
   Now beat into thine ear.

5. The gifts He gave to thee
   He gave thee to impart,
   And I too claim with thee
   His Mother and His Heart.

6. O teach me now, dear Saint,
   The secrets Christ taught thee,
   The beatings of His Heart
   And how it beat for me.

Salvete flores martyrum

1. All hail, ye lit - tle Mar - tyr Flowers, Sweet rose - buds
2. First vic - tims of the Mar - tyr bands, With crowns and
3. What prof - i - ted this great of - fence? What use was

cut in daw-ning hours: When Her - od sought the Christ to
palms in ten - der hands, A - round the ve. - ry al - tar,
Her - od's vi - o - lence? ·A Babe sur-vives that dread-ful

find, Ye fell as blooms be - fore the wind.
gay And in - no - cent, ye seem to play. A-men.
day, And Christ is safe - ly borne a - way.

4. All honor, laud and glory be,
    O Jesus, Virgin - born, to Thee;
    All glory, as is ever meet,
    To Father and to Paraclete.

NEW YEAR

Lapsus est annus: redit annus alter

1. A Year is dead, a Year is born;
2. For all past gifts we ren - der thanks,
3. O Lord, our dai - ly wants sup - ply,

Thus time flies by on si - lent wing;
For gra - ces new we hum - bly pray,
Pro - tect from sick - ness and dis - ease,

Thou Lord a - lone canst guide our course
O grant that we and those we love
And deign to give, O God of Love,

And safe to Heaven Thy peo - ple bring.
May not from faith and du - ty stray. A - men.
The bles - sing of un - bro - ken peace.

4. O blot out all our former sins
   And give us strength to fall no more;
   When fight is o'er and victory won,
   Then crown us on th' eternal shore.

5. For all the old year's sins we grieve,
   Our hearts we consecrate to Thee;
   Grant us, when all our years are sped,
   Our Heavenly Father's face to see.

HOLY NAME OF JESUS
Jesu dulcis memoria

1. Je - sus, the ve - ry thought of Thee With
2. No voice can sing, no heart can frame, Nor
3. O Hope of eve - ry con - trite heart, O

sweet - ness fills the breast; But swee - ter far Thy
can the mem - 'ry find A swee - ter sound than
Joy of all the meek, To those who fall how

face to see And in Thy pres - ence rest.
Je - sus' Name, The Sa - viour of man - kind. A-men.
kind Thou art, How good to those who seek!

But what to those who find? O this
Nor tongue nor pen can show;
The love of Jesus, what it is
None but His loved ones know.

5. Jesus, our only joy be Thou,
As Thou our prize wilt be;
O Jesus, be our glory now
And through eternity.

HOLY NAME OF JESUS
Jesu Rex admirabilis

1. O Je - sus, Lord, most migh - ty
2. When Thou art in my heart, the
3. O Je - sus, sweet - ness of the

King And Con - que - ror di - vine,
world With its vain pomp de - cays,
heart, Thou liv - ing Spring of Light,

O Sweet - ness in - fi - nite, for Whom Our
The truth shines bright, and love lights up Its
So far ex - cee - ding all de - sire, All

souls un - cea - sing pine.
rea - dy - kin - dled blaze. A - men.
joys of sense or sight:

4. O dearest Jesus, let me feel
   The fulness of Thy love,
   And cleanse mine eyes to see Thy face
   In Thy bright courts above.

5. O Jesus, brighter than the Sun,
   O Balm with healing blest,
   Of all things sweet, of all things fair,
   Thou sweetest, fairest, best.

Jesu Rex admirabilis

1. Je - sus, King o'er all a - dored, Je - sus our vic -
2. Com - ing to the faith - ful heart, Light and love Thou
3. Je - sus, Lord of pure de - light, Clean - ser of the

to - rious Lord, Sweet - ness Thou that speech tran-scends,
dost im - part; Earth's de - ceit - ful pleas - ures fall,
in - ward sight, Ev - 'ry joy Thou dost ex - cel,

Hope of earth's re - mo - test ends:
Thou a - lone art All in all. A - men.
Sweet - est love's o'er - flow - ing well.

4. Unto Thee let us repair,
   Seek Thy face with earnest prayer,
   Earnest seek Thy love to know,
   Seeking still more earnest grow.

5. Jesus, let our lips proclaim
   And our lives confess Thy Name;
   Thou our joy and portion be
   Now and in eternity.

HOLY NAME OF JESUS
Jesu decus angelicum

1. O Je - sus, Thou the Beau - ty art Of
2. Ce - les - tial sweet - ness un - al - loyed, Who
3. O dea - rest Je - sus, hear the sighs Which

An - gel Worlds a - bove; Thy Name is mu - sic
eat Thee hun - ger still, Who drink of Thee still
un - to Thee I send; To Thee mine in - most

to the heart, En - chan - ting it with love.
feel a void Which on - ly Thou canst fill. A - men.
spi - rit cries, My be - ing's hope and end.

4. Abide with us and with Thy light
   Illume the soul's abyss,
   Dispel the darkness of our night
   And fill the world with bliss,

5. O Jesus, spotless Virgin - flower,
   Our life and joy, to Thee
   Be praise, beatitude, and power
   Through all eternity.

Jesu decus angelicum

1. Je - sus, high - est Heaven's com - plete - ness,
2. Ea - ting Thee the soul may hun - ger,
3. Je - sus, all de - light ex - cee - ding,

Name of mu - sic to the ear, To the lips sur -
Drin - king still a - thirst may be, But for earth - ly
On - ly hope of heart di - stressed, Wee - ping eyes and

pas - sing sweet-ness, Wine the fain - ting heart to cheer.
food no lon - ger Nor for a - ny stream but Thee. A - men.
spi - rits blee - ding Find in Thee a place of rest.

4. Stay, O Beauty uncreated,
   Ever ancient, ever new;
   Banish clouds of darkness hated,
   With Thy sweetness all bedew.

5. Jesus, fairest Blossom, springing
   From the womb of Virgin pure,
   May our lips Thy praise be singing
   While eternal years endure.

EPIPHANY
Crudelis Herodes Deum

1. How vain the cru - el Her - od's fear When told that
2. The Eas - tern Sa - ges saw from far. And fol - lowed
3. With - in the Jor - dan's sa - cred flood The heaven - ly

Christ the King is near: He takes not earth - ly realms a -
on His gui - ding star; By light their way to Light they
Lamb in meek - ness stood, That He to Whom no sin was

way Who gives the realms that ne'er · de - cay.
trod And by their gifts con - fessed their God. A - men.
known Might cleanse His peo - ple from their own.

4. And O what miracle divine
When water reddened into wine!
He spake the word and forth it flowed
In streams that nature ne'er bestowed.

5. All glory, Jesus, be to Thee
For this Thy glad Epiphany,
Whom with the Father we adore
And Holy Ghost forevermore.

O sola magnarum urbium

1. Beth - le - hem, of no - blest ci - ties
2. Fai - rer than the sun at mor - ning
3. By its lam - bent beau - ty gui - ded,

None can once with thee com-pare; Thou a - lone the
Was the star that told His birth, To the lands their
See the Eas - tern Kings ap - pear; See them bend their

Lord from hea - ven Didst for us In - car-nate bear.
God an-noun-cing, Hid be-neath a form of earth. A-men.
gifts to of - fer, Gifts of in - cense, gold and myrrh.

4. Solemn things of mystic meaning:
Incense doth the God disclose,
Gold a royal Child proclaimeth,
Myrrh a future tomb foreshows.

5. Holy Jesus, in Thy brightness
To the Gentile world displayed,
With the Father and the Spirit,
Endless praise to Thee be paid.

37 EPIPHANY

Linquunt tecta magi principis urbis

1. The prince-ly ci-ty pas-sing by, The Ma-gi turn to greet The goal of all their toil-some march In Beth-lem's low-ly street, And, while from ma-ny tune-ful lips Spon-

2. Tran-spor-ting joy, when once a-gain The star that they had lost, With heav'n-ly light and prom-ise bright Their ea-ger path-way crossed, un-til It Nor stayed its ra-diant course.

3. No glint is here of i-vo-ry, No blaze of bur-nished gold, No pur-ple robes the in-fant limbs In gor-geous hues en-fold. His pal-ace is a sta-ble rude, His

Tune from Arundel Hymns by permission.

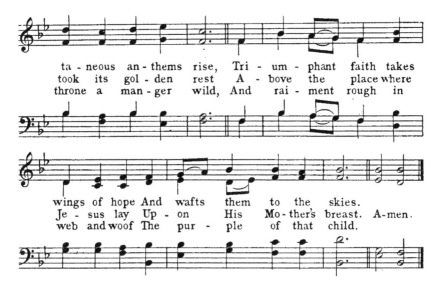

ta - neous an - thems rise, Tri - um - phant faith takes
took its gol - den rest A - bove the place where
throne a man - ger wild, And rai - ment rough in

wings of hope And wafts them to the skies.
Je - sus lay Up - on His Mo - ther's breast. A - men.
web and woof The pur - ple of that child.

4. Let pomp and splendor other kings
   Luxuriously adorn,
   For better proves He thus His reign
   Supreme, the Babe new-born.
   In peasant garb and culture mean
   He sways the realms of thought,
   And 'neath the sceptre of His will
   The hearts of men are brought.

5. Beside the cradle where He sleeps
   They worship on their knees,
   And in the Child the eye of faith
   The present Godhead sees.
   Let us, their offspring in the faith,
   Adore the Infant here,
   And offer Him our best of gifts,
   Hearts filled with sacred fear.

6. Let chaste and ardent love supply
   The gold of Eastern kings,
   And bodies penance-chastened yield
   The myrrh devotion brings.
   Our vows and pray'rs, like frankincense
   And myrrh, shall sweetly rise
   To hail the Babe recumbent here
   As Ruler of the skies.

1. They leave the land of gems and gold, The shi - ning por - tals of the East: For Him, 'the Wo - man's Seed' fore - told, They leave the rev - el and the feast.

2. To earth their scep - tres they have cast, And crowns by kings an - ces - tral worn: They track the lone - ly Syr - ian waste, They kneel be - fore the Babe new - born.

3. O hap - py eyes that saw Him first: O hap - py lips that kissed His feet: Earth slakes at last her an - cient thirst, With E - den's joy her pul - ses beat.

He, He is King, and He a - lone, Who lifts that in - fant hand to bless, Who makes His Mo - ther's knee His throne, Yet rules the star - ry wil - der - ness. A - men.

From Arundel Hymns by permission.

EPIPHANY
Jesu thronum majestatis

1. Je - sus, Who from Thy Fa - ther's throne Didst to this vale of tears come down In our poor na - ture dressed, O may the charms of that sweet love Draw up our souls to Thee a - bove And fix them there to rest.

2. Je - sus, Whose high and hum - ble Birth, In Heaven the An - gels, and on earth The faith - ful shep - herds, sing, O may our hymns, which here run low, Shoot up a - loft and fruit - ful grow In that e - ter - nal spring. A - men.

3. Je - sus, to Whom three kings from far, Led to Thy cra - dle by a star, Brought gifts to Thee their King, O may guide us by Thy light, that we May find Thy face, and un - to Thee Our - selves for trib - ute bring.

4. Jesus, Who thus began our bliss,
   Thus carried on our happiness,
   To Thee all praise be paid.
   O may the great Mysterious Three
   For ever live, and ever be
   Adored, beloved, obeyed.

1. A - gain the   time ap - poin - ted   see That
2. But vain all   out - ward form   of   grief And
3. The fore - head pros - trate in   the   dust, The

calls to   fast   and sigh, Let priest and peo - ple
vain   the   word   of   prayer, Un - less the heart de -
hair   and   gar - ments torn, Can nev - er stay the

bend   the   knee And loud for mer - cy cry.
sire   re - lief And pen - i - tence be there. A - men.
ven - geance just Un - less the   con - science mourn.

4. Great Three in One, Thy Name we bless,
   Thy praises ever sing,
   O grant that fruits of righteousness
   From Lenten tears may spring.

LENT
Audi benigne Conditor

1. Cre - a - tor boun - tecus and be - nign, With tears we pray, Thine
2. Great Searcher of the reins and heart, Thou seest us frail, Thy
3. Our sins are mul - ti - plied and great, But spare us in our

ear in - cline, As in these hal - lowed days of Lent Our
grace im - part, We turn to Thee, Thy mer - cy show And
help - less state, And for Thy Name's re - nown and praise Our

con - trite sighs to Heav'n are sent. A - men.
par - don for our sins be - stow.
souls to health and vir - tue raise.

Tune from Arundel Hymns by permission.

4. May we by wholesome penance now
Compel our sinful flesh to bow,
That, tutored in this sacred time,
Our humbled hearts may fast from crime.

5. O grant us, Blessed Three in One,
To end with fruit our course begun;
May contrite fasts and ardent love
Secure us endless joys above.

1. The dark-ness fleets and joy-ful earth Now
2. Who giv-est this ac-cept-ed time, Give
3. That foun-tain whence our sins have flowed Shall

greets the new-born day; O Thou true Sun of
tears that con-trite be, Give flames of love our
soon in tears dis-til, If but Thy pen-i-

hu-man souls, Il-lume us with Thy ray.
hearts to burn As vic-tims un-to Thee. A-men.
ten-tial grace Sub-due the stub-born will.

From Catholic Church Hymnal by permission of J. Fischer & Bro.

4. The day is near when all re-blooms,
Thy own blest day, O Lord;
We too would joy, by Thy right hand
To life's true path restored.

5. All glorious Trinity, to Thee
Let earth's vast fabric bend,
And evermore from souls renewed
The Saints' new song ascend.

LENT
Tinctum ergo Christi sanguine

1. O turn those bles - sed points, all bathed In
2. Pierce through my feet, my hands, my heart; So
3. So shall my feet be slow to sin, My

Je - sus' Blood, on me; The sins were mine that
may some drops di - stil Of Blood di - vine with-
hands shall harm - less be; So from my woun - ded

wrought His death; Be mine the pen - al - ty.
in my soul And all its e - vils heal. A - men.
heart shall each For - bid - den pas - sion flee.

4. Thee, Jesus, pierced with nails and spear,
   Let every knee adore,
   With Thee, O Father, and with Thee,
   O Spirit, evermore.

PASSION
Jesu nostros ob reatos

1. Je - sus, all hail, Who for my sin Didst
2. Je - sus, Who at this ve - ry hour At
3. Je - sus, Who shalt in glo - ry come With

die and by that Death didst win E - ter - nal life for me.
God's right hand in pomp and pow'r Our na - ture still dost wear,
An - gels to the fi - nal doom, Men's works and wills to weigh,

Send me Thy grace, good Lord, that I Un - to the world and
O let Thy Wounds still in - ter - cede And by their sim - ple
Since from that pomp I can - not flee, Be mer - ci - ful, great

flesh may die And hide my life with Thee.
si - lence plead Thy count-less mer - its there. A-men.
Lord, to me In that tre - men - dous Day.

1. O come and mourn with me a while; See, Ma - ry calls us
2. Have we no tears to shed for Him, While sol-diers scoff and
3. Seven times He spoke, seven words of love; And all three hours His

to her side; O come and let us mourn with her.
Jews de - ride? Be - hold how pa - tient - ly He hangs.
si - lence cried For mer - cy on the souls of men.

rit.

Je-sus, our Love, Je-sus, our Love, is Cru - ci - fied.
Je-sus, our Love, Je-sus, our Love, is Cru - ci - fied. A-men.
Je-sus, our Love, Je-sus, our Love, is Cru - ci - fied.

Tune from Catholic Church Hymnal by permission of J. Fischer & Bro.

4. O break, O break, hard heart of mine;
    Thy weak self-love and guilty pride
    His Pilate and His Judas were.
    Jesus, our Love, is Crucified.

5. O Love of God: O sin of man:
    In this dread act your strength is tried,
    And victory remains with Love.
    Jesus, our Love, is Crucified.

From Arundel Hymns by permission.

1. O come and mourn with me a while;
2. Have we no tears to shed for Him,
3. Seven times He spoke, seven words of love;

See, Ma-ry calls us to her side; O come and
While sol-diers scoff and Jews de-ride? Be-hold how
And all three hours His si-lence cried For mer-cy

let us mourn with her.
pa-tient-ly He hangs. } Je-sus, our Love, is Cru-ci-
on the souls of men.

fied, Je-sus, our Love, is Cru-ci-fied. A-men.

4. O break, O break, hard heart of mine;
Thy weak self-love and guilty pride
His Pilate and His Judas were.
Jesus, our Love, is Crucified.

5. O Love of God: O sin of man:
In this dread act your strength is tried,
And victory remains with Love.
Jesus, our Love, is Crucified.

PASSION

Saevo dolorum turbine

1. O'er - whelmed in depths of woe, Up -
2. See how the nails those hands And
3. O hear that last loud cry, Which

on the Tree of scorn Hangs Je - sus, Sa - viour
feet so ten - der rend; See down His face and
pierced His Mo - ther's heart, As in - to God the

of man - kind, With rack - ing an - guish torn.
neck and breast His sa - cred Blood de - scend. A-men.
Fa - ther's hands He bade His soul de - part.

4. Earth hears and trembling quakes
Around that Tree of pain,
The rocks are rent, the graves are burst,
The veil is rent in twain.

5. Shall man alone be mute?
Have we no griefs, no fears?
Come old and young, come all mankind,
And bathe those feet in tears.

6. Come, fall before His Cross
Who shed for us His Blood,
Who died the Victim of pure love
To make us sons of God.

7. O Jesus, praise to Thee,
Our joy and endless rest:
Be Thou our Guide while pilgrims here,
Our Crown amid the blest.

Prome vocem, mens, canoram

1. Slow and mourn - ful be our tone,
2. All for man the lash He bore
3. Pierced for us, a dou - ble tide

Tel - ling of the grief un - known, Grief that on the
And the thorns His tem - ples tore; Bound and help-less
Flow-eth from His pre - cious side; Aw - ful Mys-te -

Sin - less weighed When the sin - ner's debt He paid.
on the tree, Man en-slaved He set - teth free. A-men.
ries re - vere, Hail the Font and Al - tar here.

4. Blessed streams forever flow,
   Bringing grace to all below,
   Here our cup of blessing prove
   And our cup of bliss above.

5. Man of sorrows, Man of grief,
   Let us find in Thee relief,
   Till, the night of sorrow o'er,
   Sadly flows Thy praise no more.

PASSION
Salve caput cruentatum

1. O sa - cred Head, sur - roun - ded By
2. I see Thy strength and vig - or All
3. In this Thy bit - ter Pas - sion, Good

crown of pier - cing thorn, O
fa - ding in the strife, And
Shep - herd, think of me With

blee - ding Head, so woun - ded, Re -
death with cru - el rig - or Be -
Thy most sweet com - pas - sion, Un -

viled and put to scorn: Death's
rea - ving Thee of life. O
wor - thy though I be, Be -

pal - lid hue comes o'er Thee, The
ag - o - ny and dy - - ing: O
neath Thy Cross a - bi - - ding. For

glow of life de - cays, Yet An - gel hosts a -
love to sin - ners free: O Je - sus, grace sup -
ev - er would I rest, In all Thy love con -

dore Thee And trem - ble as they gaze. A-men.
ply - ing, Do turn Thy face on me.
fi - ding. And with Thy Pres - ence blest.

1. Sta - bat Ma - ter do - lo - ro - sa
2. Cu - jus a - ni - mam ge - men - tem,
3. O quam tri - stis et af - fli - cta

Ju - xta cru - cem la - cri - mo - sa,
Con - tri - sta - tam et do - len - tem,
Fu - it il - la be - ne - di - cta

Dum pen - de - bat Fi - li - us.
Per - tran - si - vit gla - di - us. A - men.
Ma - ter U - ni - ge - ni - ti!

Harmonies by Julius Bas.

4. Quæ mærebat et dolebat
   Pia Mater, dum videbat
   Nati pœnas inclyti.

5. Quis est homo qui non fleret,
   Matrem Christi si videret
   In tanto supplicio?

6. Quis non posset contristari,
   Christi Matrem contemplari
   Dolentem cum Filio?

7. Pro peccatis suæ gentis
   Vidit Jesum in tormentis,
   Et flagellis subditum.

8. Vidit suum dulcem Natum
   Moriendo desolatum,
   Dum emisit spiritum.

9. Eia Mater, fons amoris,
   Me sentire vim doloris
   Fac, ut tecum lugeam.

10. Fac ut ardeat cor meum
    In amando Christum Deum,
    Ut sibi complaceam.

11. Sancta Mater, istud agas,
    Crucifixi fige plagas
    Cordi meo valide.

12. Tui Nati vulnerati,
    Tam dignati pro me pati,
    Pœnas mecum divide.

13. Fac me tecum pie flere,
    Crucifixo condolere,
    Donec ego vixero.

14. Juxta Crucem tecum stare,
    Et me tibi sociare
    In planctu desidero.

15. Virgo virginum præclara,
    Mihi jam non sis amara;
    Fac me tecum plangere.

16. Fac ut portem Christi mortem,
    Passionis fac consortem,
    Et plagas recolere.

17. Fac me plagis vulnerari,
    Fac me Cruce inebriari,
    Et cruore Filii.

18. Flammis ne urar succensus,
    Per te, Virgo, sim defensus
    In die judicii.

19. Christe, cum sit hinc exire,
    Da per Matrem me venire
    Ad palmam victoriæ.

20. Quando corpus morietur
    Fac ut animæ donetur
    Paradisi gloria.

PASSION

Stabat Mater

1. At the Cross her sta - tion kee - ping,
2. Through her heart, His sor - row sha - ring,
3. O how sad and sore di - stres - sèd

Stood the mourn - ful Mo - ther wee - ping,
All his bit - ter an - guish bea - ring,
Was that Mo - ther ev - er Bles - sèd,

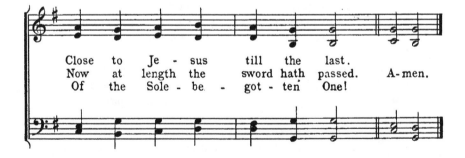

Close to Je - sus till the last.
Now at length the sword hath passed. A - men.
Of the Sole - be - got - ten One!

4. O that silent ceaseless mourning,
   Dim her eyes yet never turning
   From that wondrous suffering Son!

5. Who on Christ's dear Mother gazing
   In her trouble so amazing,
   Born of woman, would not weep?

6. Who on Christ's dear Mother thinking
   Such a cup of anguish drinking,
   Would not share her sorrow deep?

7. For His people's sins atoning,
   She saw Jesus writhing, groaning,
   'Neath the scourge wherewith He bled.

8. Her beloved One, her Consoler,
   Saw she whelmed in direst dolor
   Till at length His spirit fled.

9. Fount of love and sacred sorrow,
   Mother, may my spirit borrow
   Somewhat of thy holy woe.

10. May my heart, on fire within me
    With the love of Jesus, win me
    Grace to please Him here below.

11. Mother, every wound and tremor
    Of the Crucified Redeemer
    Firmly fasten in my soul.

12. Every shame which thou art sharing
    O divide with me unsparing,
    Every pang and pain and dole.

13. Grant that I my tears may mingle
    With thine own in sorrow single
    For my Saviour Crucified.

14. Let me, till my breath shall falter,
    Near to thee at Calvary's altar,
    Join my heart to Him Who died.

15. Queen of Virgins, best and dearest,
    Grant the prayer that now thou hearest:
    Let me ever mourn with thee.

16. Let compassion me so fashion
    That thy Son's most sacred Passion
    Daily be renewed in me.

17. Be His Wounds my own transfixion,
    May His Blood of benediction
    Ebriate my soul entire.

18. Virgin, when the mountains quiver,
    From that flame which burneth ever
    Shield me on the Day of Ire.

19. Christ, when I account must render,
    Be Thy Mother my defender,
    Be Thy Cross my victory.

20. Dust to dust itself betaking,
    May my soul enraptured waking
    Paradisal glory see.

PASSION

Pange lingua gloriosi lauream certaminis

1. Sing, my tongue, the glo - rious Bat - tle,
2. He our Ma - ker, dee - ply grie - ving
3. Thus the work for our sal - va - tion

Sing the last the dread af - fray,
That the first - made Ad - am fell,
He or - dai - ned to be done,

O'er the Cross the Vic - tor's tro - phy
When he ate the fruit for - bid - den
To the trai - tor's art op - po - sing

Sound the high tri - um - phal lay,
Whose re - ward was death and hell,
Art yet dee - per than his own,

Organ

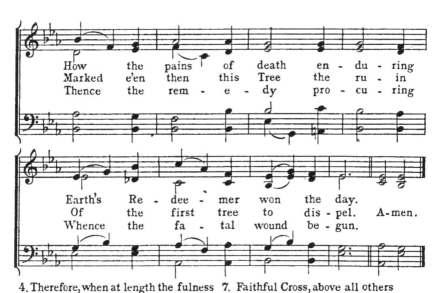

How the pains of death enduring
Marked e'en then this Tree the ruin
Thence the remedy procuring

Earth's Redeemer won the day.
Of the first tree to dispel. A-men.
Whence the fatal wound begun.

4. Therefore, when at length the fulness
Of th' appointed time was come,
He was sent, the world's Creator,
From the Father's heavenly home,
And was found in human fashion,
Offspring of the Virgin's womb.

5. Now the thirty years accomplished,
Which on earth He willed to see,
Born for this He meets His Passion,
Gives Himself an Offering free.
On the Cross the Lamb is lifted,
There the Sacrifice to be.

6. There the nails and spear He suffers,
Vinegar and gall and reed,
From His sacred Body piercèd
Blood and water both proceed;
Precious Blood, which all creation
From the stain of sin hath freed.

7. Faithful Cross, above all others
One and only noble Tree:
None in foliage, none in blossom,
None in fruit Thy peer may be.
Sweetest wood and sweetest iron,
Sweetest Weight is hung on thee.

8. Bend thy boughs, O Tree of glory,
Thy relaxing sinews bend,
For a while the ancient rigor
That thy birth bestowed suspend,
And the King of heavenly beauty
On thy bosom gently tend.

9. Thou alone wast counted worthy
This world's ransom to sustain,
That a shipwrecked race forever
Might a port of refuge gain,
With the sacred Blood anointed
Of the Lamb for sinners slain.

10. Praise and honor to the Father,
Praise and honor to the Son,
Praise and honor to the Spirit,
Ever Three and ever One,
One in might and One in glory
While eternal ages run.

PASSION

Vexilla Regis prodeunt

1. The Roy - al Ban - ners for - ward go, The
2. Where deep for us the spear was dyed, Life's
3. Ful - filled is all that Da - vid told In

Cross shines forth in mys - tic glow,
tor - rent rush - ing from His side,
true pro - phet - ic song of old;

Where He in Flesh, our flesh Who made, Our
To wash us in that pre - cious flood Where
A - midst the na - tions, God, saith he, Hath

sen - tence bore, our ran - som paid;
min - gled wa - ter flowed and Blood.
reigned and tri - umphed from the Tree.

Tune from Arundel Hymns by permission.

O faith-ful Cross, O no-blest Tree, In all our woods there's none like thee; No earth-ly groves, no sha-dy bowers, Pro-duce such leaves, such fruit, such flowers. A-men.

4. O Tree of beauty, Tree of light,
   O Tree with royal purple dight,
   Elect, on whose triumphal breast
   Those holy limbs should find their rest;
   O faithful Cross,........

5. O Cross, our one reliance, hail:
   This holy Passion-tide avail
   To give fresh merit to the saint
   And pardon to the penitent.
   O faithful Cross,........

6. On whose dear arms so widely flung
   The weight of this world's ransom hung,
   The price of humankind to pay
   And spoil the spoiler of his prey.
   O faithful Cross,........

7. To Thee eternal Three in One
   Let homage meet by all be done;
   Whom by the Cross Thou dost restore
   Preserve and govern evermore.
   O faithful Cross,........

PASSION
Consummatum est

1. It is Fin - ished. He hath seen
2. It is Fin - ished. He hath wept
3. It is Fin - ished. He hath borne

Each be - loved one leave His side;
O'er the com - ing of His woe,
Scep - tred reed and mock - ing stare,

He by one be - trayed hath been,
Till the blood in tor - rents swept
Pur - ple robe and crown of thorn,

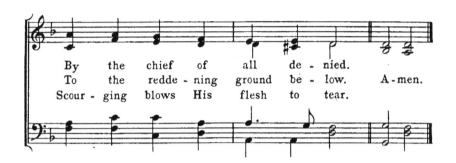

By the chief of all de - nied.
To the redde - ning ground be - low. A - men.
Scour - ging blows His flesh to tear.

4. It is Finished. He hath stood
By the ribald king, whose hand,
Guilty of the Baptist's blood,
Mocked Him to his soldier-band.

5. It is Finished. He hath bowed
'Neath the Cross to Calvary's steep,
And hath seen amidst the crowd
His belovéd Mother weep.

6. It is Finished. Not a wail
Told His pain, when hammer sent
To the very head the nail,
Through His sinews crushed and rent.

7. It is Finished. He hath hung
Three long hours in grief to die;
Curses loud on every tongue,
Malice in each heart and eye.

8. It is Finished. Naught is left.
He may yield at last His breath.
Bleeding, bruised, forlorn, bereft,
Life, in dying, conquers death.

PALM SUNDAY
Gloria, laus et honor

All glo - ry, laud and hon - or To Thee Re - dee - mer King,

To Whom the lips of chil - dren Made sweet Ho - san - nas ring.

Fine

1. Thou art the King of Is - rael, Thou Da - vid's roy - al Son, Who
2. The com - pa - ny of An - gels Are prai - sing Thee on high, And
3. The peo - ple of the Hebrews With palms be - fore Thee went; Our

D.C.

in the Lord's Name com - est, The King and Bles - sed One.
mor - tal men and all things Cre - a - ted make re - ply. A - men.
praise and prayer and an - thems Be - fore Thee we pre - sent.

4. To Thee before Thy Passion
They sang their hymns of praise;
To Thee now high exalted
Our melody we raise.
All glory....

5. Thou didst accept their praises;
Accept the prayers we bring,
Who in all good delightest,
Thou good and gracious King.
All glory....

Victimae paschali laudes

1. Christ the Lord is Risen to day: Chris-tians, haste your vows to pay.
2. Christ the Vic-tim un - de-filed Man to God hath re - con-ciled,
3. Say, O won-dering Ma - ry, say, What thou saw-est on thy way.

Of - fer ye your prai-ses meet At the Pa-schal Vic-tim's feet.
Whilst in strange and aw - ful strife Met to - ge-ther Death and Life.
I be-held, where Christ had lain, Emp-ty tomb and An - gels twain;

For the sheep the Lamb hath bled, Sin - less in the sin-ner's stead.
Chris-tians, on this hap-py day, Haste with joy your vows to pay.
I be-held the glo - ry bright Of the ri - sing Lord of Light.

Christ is risen to - day, we cry, Now He lives no more to die.
Christ is risen to - day, we cry, Now He lives no more to die. A-men.
Christ my Lord is risen a-gain, Now He lives and lives to reign.

4. Christ, Who once for sinners bled,
Now first-fruit of all the dead,
Throned in endless might and power
Lives and reigns for evermore.
Hail, eternal hope on high:
Hail, Thou King of victory:
Hail, Thou Prince of Life adored.
Help and save us, gracious Lord.

EASTER
O filii et filiae

Al - le - lu - ia!   Al - le - lu - ia!

Al - le - lu - ia!

1. O   sons and
2. In   ve - ry
3. An   An - gel

daugh - ters,   let   us   sing: The   King   of
ear - ly   mor - ning   grey   Went   ho - ly
clad   in   white   they   see,   Who   sat   and

Heaven, the glo - rious King, O'er death to -
wo - men on their way To see the
spake un - to the three: 'Your Lord hath

day rose tri - um - phing.
tomb where Je - sus lay.
gone to Ga - li - lee.'

Al - - le - lu - ia! A - men.

Alleluia! ....
4. That night th' Apostles met in fear,
But in their midst did Christ appear:
'My Peace,' saith He, 'be to you here.'
Alleluia!

Alleluia! ....
5. But Thomas, when of this he heard,
Was doubtful of his brethren's word;
Wherefore again there came the Lord.
Alleluia!

Alleluia! ....
6. 'My piercèd Side, O Thomas, see;
My Hands, My Feet, I show to thee;
Not faithless but believing be.'
Alleluia!

Alleluia! ....
7. When Thomas saw that wounded Side,
The truth no longer he denied;
'Thou art my Lord and God,' he cried.
Alleluia!

Alleluia! ....
8. O blest are they who have not seen
And yet whose faith hath constant been,
Life everlasting they shall win.
Alleluia!

Alleluia! ....
9. Now let us praise the Lord most high,
And strive His Name to magnify
This Day of days through earth and sky.
Alleluia!

(57 - 2)

EASTER

Ad regias Agni dapes

1. At the Lamb's high Feast we sing, Al - - le - lu - ia,
2. Praise we Him Whose love di - vine, Al - - le - lu - ia,
3. Where the Pas - chal Blood is poured, Al - - le - lu - ia,

Praise to our vic - to - rious King, Al - - le - lu - ia,
Gives the guests His Blood for wine, Al - - le - lu - ia,
Death's dark an - gel sheathes his sword, Al - - le - lu - ia,

Washed our gar - ments in the tide, Al - - le - lu - ia,
Gives His Bo - dy for the feast, Al - - le - lu - ia,
Is - rael's hosts tri - umphant go, Al - - le - lu - ia,

ff

Flowing from His pier-cèd side, Al - - le - lu - ia.
Love the Vic - tim, Love the Priest, Al - - le - lu - ia. A-men.
Through the wave that drowns the foe. Al - - le - lu - ia.

4. Christ the Lamb Whose Blood is shed, Alleluia,
   Paschal Victim, Paschal Bread, Alleluia.
   With sincerity and love, Alleluia,
   Eat we Manna from above, Alleluia.

5. Mighty Victim from on high, Alleluia,
   Powers of hell beneath Thee lie, Alleluia.
   Death is conquered in the fight, Alleluia,
   Thou hast brought us life and light, Alleluia.

6. Now Thy banner Thou dost wave, Alleluia,
   Vanquished Satan and the grave, Alleluia.
   Overthrown the prince of hell, Alleluia,
   Angels join Thy praise to tell, Alleluia.

7. Paschal triumph, Paschal joy, Alleluia,
   Only sin can this destroy, Alleluia.
   From the death of sin make free, Alleluia,
   Souls re-born, dear Lord, in Thee, Alleluia.

8. Hymns of glory, songs of praise, Alleluia,
   Father, unto Thee we raise, Alleluia.
   Risen Lord, all praise to Thee, Alleluia,
   Ever with the Spirit be, Alleluia.

EASTER

Chorus novae Jerusalem ----

1. Ye choirs of New Je - ru - sa - lem, Your
2. How Ju - dah's Li - on burst His chains And
3. From hell's de - vou - ring jaws the prey A -

swee - test notes em - ploy, The Pas - chal Vic - to -
crushed the ser - pent's head, And brought with Him from
lone our Lea - der bore; His ran - somed hosts pur -

ry to hymn In strains of ho - ly joy.
death's do - mains The long - im - pri - soned dead. A - men.
sue their way Where He hath gone be - fore.

4. Triumphant in His glory now,
His sceptre ruleth all,
Earth, Heaven and hell before Him bow
And at His footstool fall.

5. While joyful thus His praise we sing,
His mercy we implore,
Into His Palace bright to bring
And keep us evermore.

6. Through times unknown to earthly thought,
O Father, praise to Thee,
To Him Who our salvation wrought
And to the Spirit be.

Aurora coelum purpurat

1. The Dawn was pur - pling o'er the sky, With
2. When our most val - iant migh - ty King From
3. When He, Whom stone and seal and guard Had

al - le - lu - ias rang the air, This earth held glo - rious
death's a - byss in dread ar - ray Led long - im - pris-oned
safe - ly to the tomb con-signed, Tri - um-phant rose, and

ju - bi - lee, Hell gnashed its teeth in fierce de-spair.
Fa - thers forth In - to the beam of Life and Day. A - men.
bu - ried death Deep in the grave He left be-hind.

Tune from Catholic Church Hymnal by permission of J. Fischer & Bro.

4. Now calm your grief and still your tears,
The Angel to the mourner cries,
'For Christ is risen from the dead
And death is slain, no more to rise.'

5. O Jesus, from the death of sin
Keep us we pray, so Thou shalt be
The everlasting Paschal Joy
Of all the souls new-born in Thee.

6. To God the Father, with the Son
Who from the grave immortal rose,
And Thee, O Paraclete, be praise
While age on endless ages flows.

EASTER

Resurrectio et Vita

1. One great and fi - nal Sab - bath day, The
2. Close hid - den in the sea - lèd tomb He
3. The feet that trod the wine - press lone Go

Sun of our Sal - va - tion In death and dark - ness
wrought His peace - ful won - der, And broke the locks and
shod with wine - red ro - ses; The migh - ty hands hold

hid His ray, And in His bro - ken Tem - ple lay.
bars of doom As gen - tly as the gar - den gloom.
fast their own Deep writ in liv - ing ru - by stone;

But, ere the ho - ly night was— fled, He raised His
But Mi - chael, mailed in blin - ding— light, Came flash - ing
And from the Heart for ev - er - more His sa - cred

Bo - dy from the dead To rule the new cre -
from the heaven - ly hight, And rolled the stone a -
side, like Heav - en's door, To con - trite men un -

a - tion Of our sanc - ti - fi - ca - tion.—
sun - der And shook the world with thun - der.— A-men.
clo - ses And Wine of Life dis - po - ses.—

4. O God, Whose Son hath made away
   With death's dominion hoary,
   Unlock to them that grope and stray
   Wide avenues of endless day:
   Enrich with fruit of all desire
   The longing which Thou dost inspire;
   That we who guard His story
   May gaze upon His glory.

EASTER

Aurora coelum purpurat

1. The morn had spread her crim-son rays When rang the
2. He comes vic - to - rious from the grave, The Lord om-
3. Let hymns of joy to grief suc - ceed; We know that

skies with shouts of praise, And earth re - joiced the
ni - po-tent to save, And brings with Him to
Christ is risen in - deed; We hear His white - robed

hymn to swell That brought de-spair to van-quished hell.
light of day The Saints who long im - pris - oned lay.
An - gel's voice, And in our Ri - sen Lord re - joice.

Al - le - lu - ia! Al - le - lu - ia!
Al - le - lu - ia! Al - le - lu - ia! A - men.
Al - le - lu - ia! Al - le - lu - ia!

Tune from Arundel

4. With Christ we died, with Christ we rose,
When at the font His Name we chose.
O let not sin our robes defile
Nor turn to grief the Paschal smile.
Alleluia! Alleluia!

Hymns by permission.

Salve festa dies

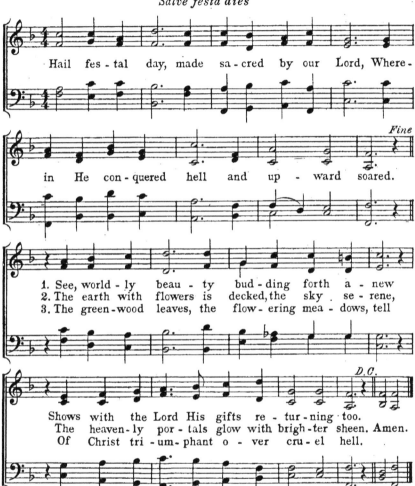

Hail fes-tal day, made sa-cred by our Lord, Where-

in He con-quered hell and up - ward soared. *Fine*

1. See, world - ly beau - ty bud - ding forth a - new
2. The earth with flowers is decked, the sky . se - rene,
3. The green - wood leaves, the flow - ering mea - dows, tell

D.C.

Shows with the Lord His gifts re - tur - ning too.
The heaven-ly por - tals glow with brigh - ter sheen. Amen.
Of Christ tri - um - phant o - ver cru - el hell.

4. The power of evil crushed, He seeks the skies:
From earth, from stars and ocean, anthems rise.
Hail festal day,......

5. The Crucified is God for evermore:
Their Maker all created things adore.
Hail festal day,......

1. Rise, glo - rious Conque - ror, rise In - to Thy
2. Li - on of Ju - dah, hail, And let Thy
3. En - ter, In - car - nate God; Thy feet have

na - tive skies; As - sume Thy right; And where in
Name pre - vail From age to age; Lord of the
more than trod The ser - pent down: Blow the full

many a fold The clouds are back - ward rolled,
rol - ling years, Claim for Thine own the spheres,
trum - pets, blow; Wi - der yon por - tals throw;

Pass through those gates of gold And reign in light.
For Thou hast bought with tears Thy her - i - tage. A-men.
Sa - viour, tri - um -phant, go And take Thy Crown.

ASCENSION
Supreme Rector coelitum

1. O King Most High of earth and sky, On pros - trate death Thou tread - est, And with Thy Blood dost mark the road Where - by to Heav'n Thou lead - est.

2. O Lord of Love, en - throned a - bove Be - side th'Al-migh - ty Fa - ther, Thou wilt not leave Thy flock to grieve, But to Thy - self wilt ga - ther. A - men.

3. O Christ, be - hold Thine or - phaned fold, Which Thou hast borne with an - guish, Steeped in the tide of Thy rent side; O leave us not to lan - guish.

.The glorious gain of all Thy pain
Henceforth Thou dost inherit;
Now comes the hour, then gently shower
On us Thy promised Spirit.

5. Dear Lord, to Thee all glory be,
Thy Father's Throne ascending:
Thy reign as One and Three shall run
Through ages never ending.

ASCENSION

Rex regum et Dominus dominantium

1. Crown Him with ma - ny crowns, The Lamb up - on His
2. Crown Him the Vir- gin's Son, The God In - car - nate
3. Crown Him the Lord of Love; Be - hold His hands and

throne; Hark how the heaven - ly an - them drowns All
born, Whose arm those crim - son tro-phies won Which
side; Rich wounds, yet vi - si - ble a - bove, In

mu - sic not its own. A - wake, my soul, and sing Of
now His brow a - dorn; Fruit of the my - stic rose, As
beau - ty glo - ri - fied. No An - gel in the sky Can

Tune from Westminster Hymnal

Him who died for thee; And hail Him as thy
of that rose the Stem; The Root whence mer - cy
ful - ly bear that sight, But down-ward bends his

match-less King Through all e - ter - ni - ty.
ev - er flows, The Babe of Beth - le - hem. A-men.
bur - ning eye At my - ste - ries so bright.

4. Crown Him the Lord of Peace,
Whose power a sceptre sways
From pole to pole, that wars may cease
Absorbed in prayer and praise.
His reign shall know no end,
And round His piercèd feet
Fair flowers of Paradise extend
Their fragrance ever sweet.

5. Crown Him the Lord of Years,
The Potentate of Time,
Creator of the rolling spheres,
Ineffably sublime,
In glazen sea of light,
Whose everlasting waves
Reflect His form, the Infinite,
Who lives and love and saves.

6. Crown Him the Lord of Heaven,
One with the Father known,
And Holy Spirit through Him given
From yonder triune throne.
All hail, Redeemer, hail,
For Thou hast died for me;
Thy praise shall never, never fail
Throughout eternity.

1. Ve - ni, Cre - a - tor Spi - ri - tus,
2. Qui di - ce - ris Pa - ra - cli - tus,
3. Tu sep - ti - for - mis mu - ne - re,

Men-tes tu - o - rum vi - si - ta: Im - ple su - per - na gra - ti - a
Al - tis - si - mi do - num De - i, Fons vi - vus, ig - nis, ca - ri - tas,
Di gitus pa-ter-næ dex-te-ræ, Tu ri - te pro - mis-sum Pa-tris,

Quae tu cre - a - sti pec - to - ra.
Et spi - ri - ta - lis unc - ti - o. A - - men.
Ser - mo - ne di - tans gut - tu - ra.

4. Accende lumen sensibus,
   Infunde amorem cordibus,
   Infirma nostri corporis
   Virtute firmans perpeti.

5. Hostem repellas longius,
   Pacemque dones protinus:
   Ductore sic te prævio,
   Vitemus omne noxium.

6. Per te sciamus da Patrem
   Noscamus atque Filium,
   Teque utriusque Spiritum
   Credamus omni tempore.

7. Deo Patri sit gloria,
   Et Filio qui a mortuis
   Surrexit, ac Paraclito,
   In sæculorum sæcula.

1. Come, O Cre - a - tor, Spi - rit blest, And in our souls take up Thy rest; Come Thou with grace and heaven-ly aid To fill the hearts which Thou hast made.

2. Great Pa - ra - clete, to Thee we cry, O high - est gift of God most high, O Fount of Life, O Fire of Love, And sol - emn Unc - tion from a - bove. A - men.

3. The sa - cred seven - fold grace is Thine, Dread Fin - ger of the Hand di - vine, The prom - ise of the Fa - ther Thou Who dost the tongue with power en - dow.

4. Our senses touch with light and fire,
Our hearts with charity inspire,
With firm endurance from on high
The weakness of our flesh supply.

5. Our enemy malign repel,
And let Thy peace within us dwell;
So may we, having Thee for Guide,
From all things hurtful turn aside.

6. O may Thy grace on us bestow
The Father and the Son to know,
And evermore to hold confessed
Thyself, of each the Spirit blest.

7. To God the Father praise be paid,
As to the Son Who from the dead
Arose, and perfect praise to Thee
O Holy Ghost, eternally.

69 PENTECOST

Beata nobis gaudia

1. Hail this joy-ful Day's re-turn, Hail the Pen-te-cos-tal morn,
2. Hear the speech be-fore unknown, Trembling crowds the won-der own;
3. Thou who didst our fa-thers guide, With their chil-dren still a-bide;

Morn when our as-cen-ded Head On His Church His Spi-rit shed.
What though hardened some a-bide, And the ho-ly work de-ride?
Grant us par-don, grant us peace, Till our earth-ly wanderings cease.

Like to clo-ven tongues of flame On the twelve the Spi-rit came;
Lord, to Thee Thy peo-ple bend, Un-to us Thy Spi-rit send;
To the Fa-ther prai-ses sing, Praise to Christ our ris-en King,

Tongues that earth may hear their call, Fire that love may burn in all.
Bles-sings of this sa-cred day Grant us, dea-rest Lord, we pray Amen.
Praise to Thee, the Lord of Love, Bles-sed Spi-rit, ho-ly Dove.

Beata nobis gaudia

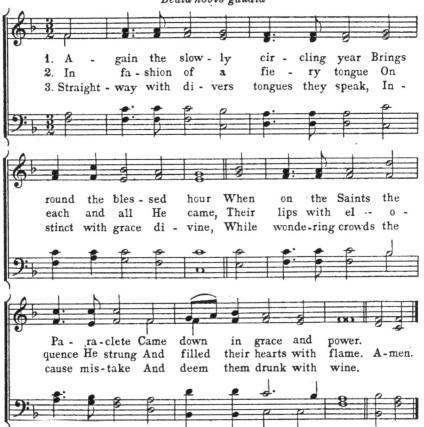

1. A - gain the slow - ly cir - cling year Brings
2. In fa - shion of a fie - ry tongue On
3. Straight - way with di - vers tongues they speak, In -

round the bles - sed hour When on the Saints the
each and all He came, Their lips with el - o -
stinct with grace di - vine, While wonde-ring crowds the

Pa - ra-clete Came down in grace and power.
quence He strung And filled their hearts with flame. A-men.
cause mis-take And deem them drunk with wine.

4. These things were mystically wrought,
The Paschal time complete,
When Israel's law remission brought
Of every legal debt.

5. O God of grace, to Thee we pray,
To Thee adoring bend;
Into our hearts, this sacred day,
Thy Spirit's fulness send.

6. Thou Who in ages past didst pour
Thy graces from above,
Thy grace in us, where lost, restore,
Establish peace and love.

7. All glory to the Father be
And to the Son Who rose;
Glory, O Holy Ghost, to Thee,
While age on ages flows.

1. Ve - ni, San - cte Spi - ri - tus, Et e - mit - te
2. Con - so - la - tor op - ti - me, Dul - cis ho - spes
3. O lux be - a - tis - si - ma, Re - ple cor - dis

coe - li - tus Lu - cis tu - ae ra - di - um.
a - ni - mae, Dul - ce re - fri - ge - ri - um.
in - ti - ma, Tu - o - rum fi - de - li - um.

Ve - ni pa - ter pau - pe - rum, Ve - ni da - tor
In la - bo - re re - qui - es, In ae - stu tem -
Si - ne tu - o nu - mi - ne, Ni - hil est in

mu - ne - rum, Ve - ni lu - men cor - di - um.
pe - ri - es, In fle - tu so - la - ti - um. A - men.
ho - mi - ne, Ni - hil est in - no - xi - um.

4. Lava quod est sordidum,
Riga quod est aridum,
Sana quod est saucium.
Flecte quod est rigidum,
Fove quod est frigidum,
Rege quod est devium.

5. Da tuis fidelibus,
In te confidentibus,
Sacrum septenarium.
Da virtutis meritum,
Da salutis exitum,
Da perenne gaudium.

Veni Sancte Spiritus

1. Come, Thou Ho - ly Spi - rit, come, And from Thy ce -
2. Com - for - ter art Thou the best, Thou the soul's most
3. O most bles - sed Light Di - vine, Shine with - in these

les - tial home Shed a ray of Light di - vine.
wel - come guest, Sweet re - fresh - ment here be - low.
hearts of Thine, And our in - most be - ing fill.

Come, Thou Fa - ther of the poor, Come, Thou Source of
In our la - bor rest most sweet, Grate - ful cool - ness
Where Thou art not man hath naught, No - thing good in

all our store, Come, with - in our bo - soms shine.
in the heat, Sol - ace in the midst of woe. A - men.
deed or thought, No - thing free from taint of ill.

4. Heal our wounds, our strength renew,
On our dryness pour Thy dew,
Wash the stains of guilt away.
Bend the stubborn heart and will,
Melt the frozen, warm the chill,
Guide the steps that else would stray.

5. On the faithful, who adore
And confess Thee evermore,
In Thy sevenfold gifts descend.
Give them virtue's sure reward,
Give them Thy salvation, Lord,
Give them joys that never end.

73

PENTECOST

Qui procedis ab utroque

1. Spi - rit of Grace and U - ni - on, Who from the Fa-ther and the Son Dost e - qual - ly pro-ceed, In - flame our hearts with ho - ly fire, Our lips with el - o - quence in - spire And streng - then us in need.

2. O in - ex - haus - tive Fount of Light, How doth Thy ra-diance put to flight The dark - ness of the mind. The pure are on - ly pure through Thee, Thou on - ly dost the guil - ty free And cheer with light the blind. A-men.

3. Thou to the low - ly dost dis - play The beau - ti - ful and per - fect way Of jus - tice and of peace; Thou to the sim - ple dost im - part What lacks the proud and stub - born heart, True wis - dom's rich in - crease.

Tune from Arundel Hymns by permission.

4. O Soo-ther of the trou-bled heart, At Thy ap - proach all
5. Thy grace e - ter-nal truth in-stils, The ig - no - rant with
6. O Thou the wea - ry pil-grim's Rest, Sol - ace of all that

cares de-part And mel - an-cho - ly grief. More
know - ledge fills, A - wa - kens those who sleep, In -
are op - pressed, Be - frien - der of the poor: O

bal - my than the sum-mer breeze, Thy pres-ence lulls all
spires the tongue, in - forms the eye, Ex - pands the heart with
Thou in Whom the wret - ched find A sweet Con - so - ler

ag - o - nies And lends a sweet re - lief.
cha - ri - ty And com - forts all who weep. A-men.
ev - er kind, A Ref - uge ev - er sure.

75

PENTECOST

Qui procedis ab utroque: Pars III

7. Spi - rit of Ho - li - ness and Might, Il -
8. And as Thou didst in days of old On
9. So un - to Thee, Who with the Son And

lu - mi - nate us with Thy Light, Thy peace on us be-stow,
ear - liest Shep-herds of the Fold In tongues of flame de-scend,
Fa - ther art for ev - er One, The Lord of earth and Heav'n,

Help us to gain the heavenly prize, And for its glo - ry
Now al - so on its Pas - tors shine And fill with fire of
Be through e - ter - nal length of days All hon - or, glo - ry,

to de - spise The world and all be - low.
grace di - vine The world from end to end. A-men.
bles - sing, praise And a - do - ra - tion given.

Tune from Arundel Hymns by permission.

1. Ho - ly God - head, One in Three,
2. Light of light, with mor - ning - shine
3. God of Peace, when falls the even,

Ru - ler of the earth and sea,
Pour on us Thy Light di - vine,
Let it close on sin for - given,

Hear us while we lift to Thee
And let cha - ri - ty be - nign
Fold us in the peace of Heaven,

Ho - ly chant and psalm.
Breathe on us her balm. A - men.
Shed a ho - ly calm.

Tune from
Catholic Hymns

4. Holy Godhead, One in Three,
Dimly here we worship Thee;
With the Saints hereafter we
Hope to bear the palm.

Cary & Co.
Publishers, London.

MOST HOLY TRINITY
Aeterna lux Divinitas

1. O Thou Im - mor - tal Light Di - vine, Blest
2. Fa - ther in maj - es - ty en - throned, We
3. As from. the Fa - ther In - cre - ate His

Tri - ni - ty in U - ni - ty, Al - migh - ty One, Al-
Thee con - fess with Christ Thy Son. Thee, Ho - ly Ghost, e -
Son and Word E - ter - nal came, So too from Each the

migh - ty Trine, Give ear to Thy cre - a - tion's cry.
ter - nal Bond Of Love u - ni - ting Both in One. A - men.
Pa - ra - clete Pro - ceeds, in De - i - ty the same.

4. Three Persons, Whom among is none
Of greater majesty or less,
In substance, essence, nature, One,
Equal in might and holiness:

5. Three Persons, One Immensity
Encircling utmost space and time,
One Greatness, Glory, Sanctity,
One everlasting Truth sublime:

6. O Thou Most Holy, wise and just,
O Lord of nature, God of grace,
Grant that as now in Thee we trust
So may we see Thee face to face.

7. Thou art the Fount of all that is,
Thou art our Origin and End,
On Thee alone our future bliss
And perpetuity depend.

8. Thou solely didst the worlds create,
Subsisting still by Thy decree,
Thou art the Light, the Glory great
And Prize of all who hope in Thee.

9. To Father, Son and Holy Ghost,
Triunal Lord of earth and Heaven
From earth and from the Heavenly Host
Be sempiternal glory given.

O luce qui mortalibus

1. In the Light all light ex - cel - ling,
2. An - gels veil their ra - diant fa - ces;
3. Watch till night is turned to mor - ning,

Light that dar - kens mor - tal eye,
Saints are trem - bling in Thy sight;
Mor - ning of th'e - ter - nal Day;

Thou, Su - preme, hast fixed Thy___ dwel - ling,
We the while, in earth's dark__ pla - ces,
Suns our earth - ly heaven a - dor - ning

Ev - er - las - ting Tri - ni - ty.
Watch the slow - ly wa - ning night; A-men.
Fade like star - light from its ray.

Tune from Catholic Hymns, by permission of Messrs. Cary & Co., publishers, London.

4. Grant that here Thy gifts receiving,
   We may there Thy glory see;
   Gazing then, no more believing,
   Trinity in Unity.

MOST HOLY TRINITY
Te Deum laudamus

1. Ho - ly God, we praise Thy Name,
2. Hark, the loud ce - les - tial hymn
3. Lo, the A - po - sto - lic train

Lord of all, we bow be - fore Thee;
An - gel Choirs a - bove are rai - sing;
Join Thy sa - cred Name to hal - low,

All on earth Thy scep - tre claim,
Cher - u - bim and Ser - a - phim
Proph - ets swell the loud re - frain

All in Heaven a - bove a - dore Thee;
In un - cea - sing cho - rus prai - sing
And the white - robed Mar - tyrs fol - low,

In - fi - nite Thy vast do - main,
Fill the Heavens with sweet ac - cord:
And from morn till set of sun

Ev - er - las - ting is Thy reign.
Ho - ly, Ho - ly, Ho - ly Lord. A-men.
Through the Church the song goes on.

4. Holy Father, Holy Son,
   Holy Spirit, Three we name Thee,
   Though in Essence only One
   Undivided God we claim Thee,
   And adoring bend the knee
   While we own the Mystery.

5. Thou art King of Glory, Christ,
   Son of God yet born of Mary,
   For us sinners sacrificed
   And to death a tributary
   First to break the bars of death,
   Thou hast opened Heaven to faith.

6. From Thy high Celestial Home,
   Judge of all, again returning,
   We believe that Thou shalt come
   In the dreadful Doomsday Morning,
   When Thy Voice shall shake the earth
   And the startled dead come forth.

7. Spare Thy people, Lord, we pray,
   By a thousand snares surrounded,
   Keep us free from sin to-day,
   Never let us be confounded:
   Lo, I put my trust in Thee,
   Never, Lord, abandon me.

HOLY EUCHARIST

Sacris solemniis juncta sint gaudia

1. Let old things pass a - way, Let all be fresh and bright, And wel - come we with hearts re - newed This feast of new de - light.
2. Up - on this hal - lowed eve Christ with His breth-ren ate, O - be - dient to the ol - den law, The Pasch be - fore Him set. A-men.
3. Which done, Him - self en - tire, The true In - car - nate God, A - like on each, a - like on all, His sa - cred hands be-stowed.

Tune reprinted by permission of the Missionary Society of St. Paul the Apostle of the State of New York.

4. He gave His Flesh, He gave
His Precious Blood, and said:
'Receive and drink ye all of this
For your salvation shed.'

5. Thus did the Lord appoint
This Sacrifice sublime,
And made His priests its ministers
Through all the bounds of time.

6. Farewell to types; henceforth
We feed on Angels' Food;
The humble servant eats the Flesh
Of his Incarnate God.

7. O blessed Three in One,
Visit our hearts we pray,
And lead us on through Thine own paths
To Thy eternal Day.

O Esca viatorum

1. O Food that wea - ry pil-grims love, O Bread of An - gel
2. O Fount of Love, O clean-sing Tide, Which from the Sa - viour's
3. Lord Je - sus, Whom by power di - vine Now hid be - neath the

Hosts a - bove, O Man-na of the Saints, The hun - gry soul would
pier - ced side And Sa-cred Heart dost flow, Thy quickening Stream be
out-ward sign We wor-ship and a - dore, Grant, when the veil a -

feed on Thee, May ne'er the heart un - sol-aced be Which
ours to share Whose boun - ty fil - leth eve - ry prayer And
way is rolled, With o - pen face may we be - hold Thy -

for Thy sweet-ness faints, Which for Thy sweet-ness faints.
need of man be - low. And need of man be - low. A-men.
self for ev - er - more. Thy - self for ev - er - more.

82

HOLY EUCHARIST
Verbum supernum prodiens

Tune from Catholic Hymns by permission of Cary & Co. Publishers, London

1. Word of God to earth de - scen - ding,
2. Well the trai - tor's kiss fore - know - ing,
3. Ho - ly Bo - dy, Blood all Pre - cious,

With the Fa - ther pres - ent still,
Mi - ra - cle of love di - vine,
Given by Him to be our Food,

Near His earth - ly jour - ney's en - ding,
See His hands Him - self be - stow - ing
With them both He doth re - fresh us,

Hastes His mis - sion to ful - fil.
In the hal - lowed Bread and Wine. A - men.
Formed like Him of flesh and blood.

4. Mighty Victim, earth's salvation,
Heavenly gates unfolding wide,
Help Thy people in temptation,
Feed them from Thy bleeding side.

5. Unto Thee the Hidden Manna,
Father, Spirit, unto Thee
Let us raise the loud Hosanna,
And adoring bend the knee.

1. Th'E - ter - nal Word, that still on high In glo - ry
2. He, by a com - rade un - to death Soon to His
3. To them in two - fold Sa - cra - ment His Blood, His

keeps the Fa - ther's side, Choo-sing to toil and weep and
foes to be be - trayed, First to the few that kept Him
Bo - dy did He give, That by a dou - ble nou - rish-

die, Came to His life's lone e - ven - tide.
faith Him - self be - trayed as Liv - ing Bread. A-men.
ment Bo - dy and soul for ay may live.

4. At birth He gives Himself, our mate:
At table gives, and lo, we eat:
Dying, He gives our ransom-price:
Reigning, He gives us Paradise.

5. O Victim of our soul's release,
Flinging celestial portals wide,
Our foes would rob us of Thy peace,
Bring aid and turn the battle's tide.

6. So from the welter and the strife
Praise to the Triune God be given,
And may He grant unending life,
Bringing us all safe home to Heaven.

HOLY EUCHARIST

Pange lingua gloriosi Corporis mysterium

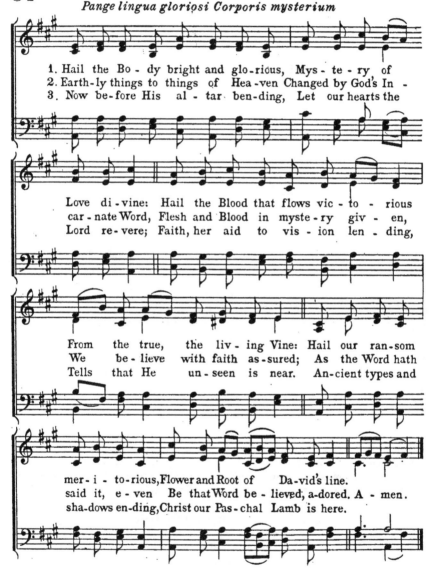

1. Hail the Bo - dy bright and glo-rious, Mys - te - ry of
2. Earth-ly things to things of Hea -ven Changed by God's In -
3. Now be-fore His al - tar bend-ing, Let our hearts the

Love di - vine: Hail the Blood that flows vic - to - rious
car - nate Word, Flesh and Blood in myste - ry giv - en,
Lord re - vere; Faith, her aid to vis - ion len - ding,

From the true, the liv - ing Vine: Hail our ran-som
We be - lieve with faith as-sured; As the Word hath
Tells that He un - seen is near. An-cient types and

mer - i - to-rious, Flower and Root of Da-vid's line.
said it, e - ven Be that Word be - lieved, a-dored. A - men.
sha-dows en-ding, Christ our Pas-chal Lamb is here.

Pange lingua gloriosi

1. On the night of that Last Sup-per, Sea-ted with His
2. Word made Flesh, the bread of na-ture By His word to
3. Down in a - do - ra - tion fal-ling, Now the Sa - cred

cho - sen band, He the Pas-chal vic-tim ea-ting
Flesh He turns, Wine in - to His Blood He chan-ges;
Host we hail: While o'er an-cient forms de-par-ting

First ful - fils the law's com-mand, Then as Food to
What though sense no change dis-cerns? On - ly be the
New - er rites of grace pre-vail; Faith for all de-

Organ

all His breth-ren Gives Him-self with His own Hand.
heart in ear - nest, Faith her les - son quick-ly learns. A-men.
fects sup-ply -ing Where the fee - ble sen-ses fail.

HOLY EUCHARIST
Ave sacer Christi sanguis

1. Hail true Blood of Je - sus, giv - en
2. Hail thou Cha - lice of Sal - va - tion:
3. In the Tor - rent ru - by - glow - ing,

To our pil - grim hearts, that Hea - ven
Nev - er had an - oth - er na - tion
From the Sa - viour's side out - flow - ing,

May be ours and end - less bliss.
Such a won - drous gift as this. A - men.
May my sins be washed a - way.

Tune from Arundel Hymns by permission.

4. Save me Lord from evil-doing:
Let me taste the joy ensuing
In the Land of endless Day.

1. Hail true Blood of Je - sus, giv - en
2. Hail thou Cha - lice of Sal - va - tion:
3. In the Tor - rent ru - by - glow - ing,

To our pil - grim hearts, that Hea - ven
Nev - er had an - oth - er na - tion
From the Sa - viour's side out - flow - ing,

May be ours and end - less bliss.
Such a won - drous gift as this. A - men.
May my sins be washed a - way.

Tune from Arundel Hymns by permission.

4. Save me Lord from evil-doing:
Let me taste the joy ensuing
In the Land of endless Day.

HOLY EUCHARIST
Ave vivens Hostia

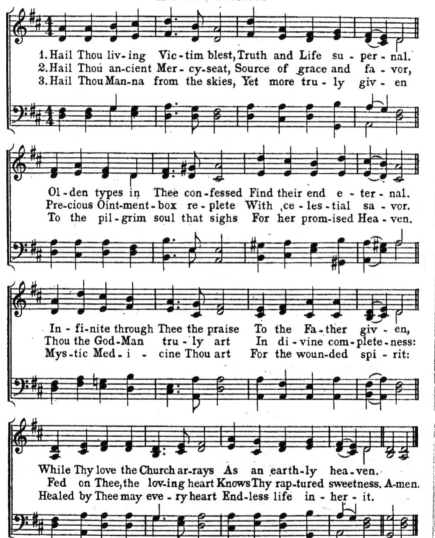

1. Hail Thou liv-ing Vic-tim blest, Truth and Life su - per - nal.
2. Hail Thou an-cient Mer - cy-seat, Source of grace and fa - vor,
3. Hail Thou Man-na from the skies, Yet more tru - ly giv - en

Ol - den types in Thee con-fessed Find their end e - ter - nal.
Pre-cious Oint-ment- box re - plete With ce - les - tial sa - vor.
To the pil - grim soul that sighs For her prom-ised Hea - ven.

In - fi-nite through Thee the praise To the Fa - ther giv - en,
Thou the God-Man tru - ly art In di - vine com-plete-ness:
Mys-tic Med - i - cine Thou art For the woun-ded spi - rit:

While Thy love the Church ar-rays As an earth-ly hea-ven.
Fed on Thee, the lov-ing heart Knows Thy rap-tured sweetness. A-men.
Healed by Thee may eve - ry heart End-less life in - her - it.

1. O Je - sus Christ, re - mem - ber, When Thou shalt come a - gain
2. Re - mem - ber then, O Sav - iour, I sup - pli - cate of Thee,
3. Ac - cept, Di - vine Re - dee - mer, The hom - age of my praise,

Up - on the clouds of hea - ven With all Thy shi - ning train,
That here I bowed be - fore Thee Up - on my ben - ded knee,
Be Thou the light and hon - or And glo - ry of my days.

When ev - ery eye shall see Thee In maj - es - ty re - vealed,
That here I owned Thy Pres - ence And did not Thee de - ny,
Be Thou my con - so - la - tion When death is draw - ing nigh,

Who now up - on this al - tar In si - lence art con - cealed.
And glo - ri - fied Thy great-ness Though hid from human eye. A - men.
Be Thou my on - ly Trea-sure Through all e - ter - ni - ty.

Tune from Catholic Church Hymnal by permission of J. Fischer & Bro.

HOLY EUCHARIST
Benedicite omnia opera Domini Domino

1. Come, all ye crea-tures of the Lord Of
2. Break forth in song, ye Se - ra - phim, True
3. Ye Pa - tri - archs of a - ges old And

high or low de - gree; Come hith - er and with
hearts with zeal a - fire; Ye Prince-doms,Thrones and
Proph - ets great and small, Ye Vir - gins pure as

one ac - cord What hath be - fal - len see.
Che - ru - bim, Your sweet - est an - them choir.
O - phir gold And twelve A - pos - tles all,

It is the Sa - cra - ment of Love That
Do - mi - nions, Vir - tues, Powers, com - bine With
Con - fes - sors too and Mar - tyrs brave, Ye

all   must bless, be - low,   a - bove: Short
An - gels all in or - ders nine,   To
Heaven - ly Hosts re - vered and   grave, Praise

rit.

be my life or long, 'Tis this shall tune my song.
bless and ev - er - more This Sa - cra - ment a - dore. A-men.
God and ev - er - more This Sa - cra - ment a - dore.

4. Ye sun and moon and stars on high
   That light the firmament,.
   Our common Master magnify
   Here in this Sacrament.
   Both hill and valley, fruit and seed,
   With greenwood tree and grassy mead,
   Praise God and evermore
   Your Maker's love adore.

5. Ye fish in flood, ye beasts afield
   And birds aloft on wing,
   Praise Him throughout the world and yield
   Due homage to your King:
   'Tis God Himself, the Son divine,
   Disguised in forms of bread and wine.
   Him therefore evermore,
   Come, worship and adore.

6. Now let the faithful, old and young,
   Sing hymns with heart and voice,
   By every tongue His praise be sung
   Till heaven itself rejoice..
   This is the Bread which Jesus saith
   Shall save mankind from endless death:
   We therefore more and more
   This Sacrament adore. ·

Adoro te devote

1. Hum - bly I a - dore Thee, Hid - den De - i - ty,
2. Taste and touch and vis - ion are de - ceived in Thee,
3. On the Cross was hid - den but Thy De - i - ty;

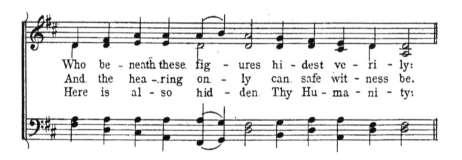

Who be - neath these fig - ures hi - dest ve - ri - ly:
And the hea - ring on - ly can safe wit - ness be.
Here is al - so hid - den Thy Hu - ma - ni - ty:

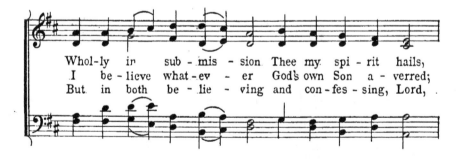

Whol - ly in sub - mis - sion Thee my spi - rit hails,
I be - lieve what - ev - er God's own Son a - verred;
But in both be - lie - ving and con - fes - sing, Lord,

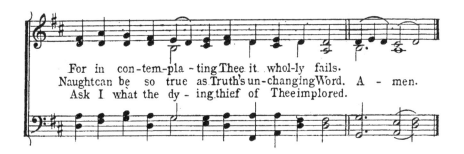

For in con-tem-pla - ting Thee it whol-ly fails.
Naught can be so true as Truth's un-changing Word. A - men.
Ask I what the dy - ing thief of Thee implored.

4. Though Thy wounds, as Thomas saw, I see not now,
   Thee my lips shall ever Lord and God avow.
   Grant that I may ever more and more believe,
   Hope in Thee and love Thee passing all reprieve.

5. O Memorial blessèd of the Saviour's death,
   O true Bread that giveth man his vital breath,
   Let my longing bosom feed on Thee alone,
   And my heart for ever but Thy sweetness own.

6. Pelican most tender, Jesus, Lord and God,
   Wash my guilty spirit in Thy Precious Blood,
   Whose one drop availeth all the world to win
   From its ban of bondage and its stain of sin.

7. Jesus, Whom thus veilèd see I here below,
   Grant, I pray, the blessing that I long for so,
   That, the veil once riven, in Thy fond embrace
   I may see Thy glory ever face to face.

HOLY EUCHARIST

Adoro te devote

1. Hum-bly I___ a - dore Thee, Hid-den De - i -
2. Taste and touch and vis - ion are de - ceived in
3. On the Cross was hid - den but Thy De - i -

ty, Who be - neath these fig - ures hi - dest
Thee, And the hea - ring on - ly can safe
ty; Here is al - so hid - den Thy Hu -

ve - ri - ly: Whol - ly in sub - mis - sion
wit - ness be. I be - lieve what-ev - er
ma - ni - ty: But in both be - lie - ving

Thee my spi - rit hails, For in con - tem -
Gods own Son a - verred; Naught can be so
and con - fes - sing, Lord, Ask I what the

pla - ting Thee it whol - ly fails.
true as Truth's un - chang - ing Word. A - - - - men.
dy - ing thief of Thee im - plored.

4. Though Thy wounds, as Thomas saw, I see not now,
   Thee my lips shall ever Lord and God avow.
   Grant that I may ever more and more believe,
   Hope in Thee and love Thee passing all reprieve.

5. O Memorial blessèd of the Saviour's death,
   O true Bread that giveth man his vital breath,
   Let my longing bosom feed on Thee alone,
   And my heart for ever but Thy sweetness own.

6. Pelican most tender, Jesus, Lord and God,
   Wash my guilty spirit in Thy Precious Blood,
   Whose one drop availeth all the world to win
   From its ban of bondage and its stain of sin.

7. Jesus, Whom thus veilèd see I here below,
   Grant, I pray, the blessing that I long for so,
   That, the veil once riven, in Thy fond embrace
   I may see Thy glory ever face to face.

93

HOLY EUCHARIST
Lauda Sion Salvatorem

1. Si - on, thy Re - dee - mer prai - sing,
2. Sing to - day, the mys - tery show - ing
3. Loud and clear ring out thy chan - ting,

Songs and hymns most glad - some rai - sing,
Of the Liv - ing life - be - stow - ing
Joy nor sweet - est grace be wan - ting,

Laud thy Pas - tor, Prince and Guide.
Bread from Heaven be - fore thee set;
To thy heart and soul to - day,

Tune from Arundel Hymns by permission.

Swell thy notes full high and da - ring,
E'en the same of old pro - vi - ded,
While we ga - ther up the mea - sure

For His praise is past de - cla - ring
Where the twelve di - vine - ly gui - ded
Of that Sup - per and its Trea - sure,

And thy lof - tiest powers be - side. A - men.
At the ho - ly ta - ble met.
Kee - ping feast in glad ar - ray.

4. Christ our King, by consecration
   Of the newer law's oblation,
   Ends the ancient Paschal rite.
   Olden forms New Substance chaseth,
   Typic shadows Truth displaceth,
   Day dispelleth darksome night.

5. What He did at Supper seated,
   Christ enjoined to be repeated
   When His love we celebrate.
   Thus, obeying His dictation,
   Bread and wine of our salvation
   We the Victim consecrate.

Lauda Sion, Pars II

6. This the truth to Chris - tians giv - en,
7. Un - der - neath the spe - cies du - al,
8. Who - so ea - teth It can nev - er

Bread be - comes His Flesh from Hea - ven,
Signs not things, is hid a Jew - el
Break the Bo - dy, rend nor sev - er;

Wine be - comes His Pre - cious Blood:
Far be - yond cre - a - tion's reach.
Christ en - tire our hearts doth fill.

Tune from Arundel Hymns by permission.

Though we feel it not nor see it,
Though His Flesh as food abideth
Multitudes this Banquet sharing,

Living Faith that doth decree it
And His Blood as drink, He hideth
Each with all as one comparing,

All defects of sense makes good.
Undivided under each. A-men.
Christ though eaten bideth still.

9. Good and bad they come to greet Him:
Unto life the former eat Him
And the latter unto death.
These find death and those find Heaven.
Lo, from one same Life-Seed given
How the harvest differeth!

10. Though the Sacrament ye sever,
In each Part endureth ever
What the Whole contained before.
In the sign though change obtaineth,
The Reality remaineth
Ever Perfect as of yore.

(94-2)

Lauda Sion. Pars III. Ecce panis angelorum
Tune from Arundel Hymns by permission.

11. Hail, An - gel - ic Bread of Hea - ven,
12. Through pro - phet - ic signs nar - ra - ted,

Now be-come the Pil - grim's Lea - ven, Bread of Life to
Once as I - saac im - mo - la - ted, By the Pas - chal

chil - dren giv - en, That to dogs must not be thrown,
Lamb pre - da - ted, In the ol - den Man - na known,

That to dogs must not be thrown.
In the ol - den Man - na known. A - men.

13. Living Bread, Good Pastor, tend us; 14. Thou Who all things canst and knowest,
   Jesus, of Thy love befriend us;   Who Thyself as Food bestowest,
   Thou refresh us, Thou defend us;   Make us, where Thy face Thou showest,
   Thy surpassing Treasures lend us   With Thy Saints, though least and lowest,
   In the Land of Life to see.   Guests and fellow - heirs to be.

1. Soul of my Sa - viour, sanc - ti - fy my breast;
2. Strength and pro - tec - tion may His Pas - sion be;
3. Guard and de - fend me from the foe ma - lign;

Bo - dy of Christ, be Thou my sa - ving guest;
O bles - sed Je - sus, hear and an - swer me;
In death's dread mo - ments make me on - ly Thine;

Blood of my Sa - viour, bathe me in Thy tide;
Deep in Thy Wounds, Lord, hide and shel - ter me;
Call me and bid me come to Thee on high,

Wash me, ye wa - ters gush - ing from His side.
So shall I nev - er, nev - er, part from Thee. A - men.
Ev - er with Saints my Lord to mag - ni - fy.

Tune from Catholic Church Hymnal by permission of J. Fischer & Bro.

HOLY EUCHARIST
Hymn before Communion

1. Haste my soul, in fash - ion nea - test
2. In His pres ence, pas - sing mea - sure,
3. Where - fore rise and run to meet Him

Deck thee ere the Bride - groom come,
There is joy and cha - ri - ty,
Ere be - fore the door He stand;

Sweep the house in man - ner mee - test,
And His friend - ship bring - eth plea - sure;
Soul, make rea - dy now to greet Him,

In thy heart pre - pare Him room.
Al - to - ge - ther love - ly He.
Pu - ri - fy thee, heart and hand.

Soon shalt thou re - ceive a Guest,
At thy house He fain would stay,
Hol - ding, see thou hold Him fast,

Gen - tlest, mee - kest, bra - vest, best;
Break His jour - ney there to - day,
Let Him not de - part in haste.

Soon to thee there shall be giv - en
Sit and rest be - neath thy ga - ble,
Cords of love be thine to bind Him

Christ, the ve - ry Bread of Hea-ven.
Eat and drink with thee at ta - ble. A-men.
Till He bles - sing leave be - hind Him.

HOLY EUCHARIST

Ubi thesaurus ibi cor

1. Lord, Thou Thy - self hast said this gol - den word:
2. Sil - ver and gold, and eve - ry pre - cious thing
3. What can I wish for on this earth be - low?

'Wher - e'er thy trea - sure, there thy heart shall be.'
That thief can steal or moth and rust con - sume,
What can I wish for in the heavens a - bove?

Here at Thy feet, my Eu - cha - ris - tic Lord,
Not to such fra - gile flee - ting goods I cling;
Heaven in this Ho - ly Mys - te - ry I know;

The mea - ning of the word grows plain to me.
For trea - sures in - fi - nite my heart hath room.
Here at the al - tar I have all I love.

Thou art my Trea - sure, Je - sus, and with
Thou art my Trea - sure, Je - sus, and with
Thou art my Trea - sure, Je - sus, and with

Thee My heart must be.
Thee My heart must be. A - men.
Thee My heart must be.

4. This altar is the school where I am taught
To hear Thy word and love Thy holy law.
Here in Thy Heart sweet modesty is sought,
Fervor and charity I hence may draw.
Thou art my Treasure, Jesus, and with Thee
My heart must be.

5. Thrice happy he who gazes thus on Thee
Before Thy altar dwelling night and day.
Such happiness as that is not for me;
But, when I leave, my love behind will stay.
Thou art my Treasure, Jesus, and with Thee
My heart must be.

99

HOLY EUCHARIST
Children's Hymn after Communion

1. Je - sus, gen - tlest Sa - viour,
2. Na - ture can not hold Thee,
3. Je - sus, gen - tlest Sa - viour,

God of might and power, Thou Thy - self art
Heaven is all too strait For Thine end - less
Thou art in us now, Fill us full of

rit.

dwel - ling In us at this hour.
glo - ry And Thy roy - al state. A - men.
good - ness Till our hearts o'er - flow.

4. O how can we thank Thee
For a gift like this?
Gift that truly maketh
Heaven's eternal bliss.

5. And when wilt Thou always
Make our hearts Thy home?
We must wait for Heaven,
Then the day will come.

1. A - do - ro te de - vo - te, la - tens De - i - tas,
2. Je - su, quem ve - la - tum nunc a - spi - ci - o,

Quae sub his fi - gu - ris ve - re la - ti - tas.
O - ro fi - at il - lud quod tam si - ti - o,

Ti - bi se cor me - um to - tum sub - ji - cit;
Ut te re - ve - la - ta cer - nens fa - ci - e

Qui - a te con - tem - plans to - tum de - fi - cit.
Vi - su sim be - a - tus tu - ae glo - ri - ae. A - men.

Harmonies by Julius Bas

101 HOLY EUCHARIST
Hymn at Exposition

1. A-do-ro te de-vo-te, la-tens De-i-tas,
2. Je-su, quem ve-la-tum nunc a-spi-ci-o,

Quae sub his fi-gu-ris ve-re la-ti-tas. Ti-bi
O-ro fi-at il-lud quod tam si-ti-o, Ut te

se cor me-um to-tum sub-ji-cit, Qui-a
re-ve-la-ta cer-nens fa-ci-e, Vi-su

te con-tem-plans to-tum de-fi-cit. A - - men.
sim be-a-tus tu-ae glo-ri-ae.

Hymn at Exposition

1. A - ve ve - rum Cor - pus, na - tum
2. Cu - jus la - tus per - fo - ra - tum

Ex Ma - ri - a Vir - gi - ne, Ve - re pas - sum,
Flu - xit a - qua et san - gui - ne, Es - to 'no - bis

im - mo - la - tum In cru - ce pro ho - mi - ne,
prae - gu - sta - tum Mor - tis in e - xa - mi - ne,

Je - su Fi - li Ma - ri - ae. A - men.

Tune from Arundel Hymns by permission.

HOLY EUCHARIST
Hymn at Exposition

A - ve ve - rum Cor - pus, na - tum

Ex Ma - ri - a vir - gi - ne,— Ve - re pas - sum

im - mo - la - tum In cru - ce pro ho - mi - ne.—

Cu - jus la - tus per - fo - ra - tum

Flu - xit a - qua et, san - gui - ne, Es - to no - bis

prae - gu - sta - tum Mor - tis in ex -

a - mi - ne. O cle - mens, O pi - e,

O dul - cis Je - su Fi - li Ma - ri - ae. A - men.

Tune from Arundel Hymns by permission.

HOLY EUCHARIST
Hymn at Exposition

1. A - ve ve - rum Cor - pus, na - tum
2. Cu - jus la - tus per - fo - ra - tum

Ex Ma - ri - a vir - gi - ne,
Flu - xit a - qua et san - gui - ne,

Ve - re pas - sum im - mo - la - tum
Es - to no - bis prae - gu - sta - tum

HOLY EUCHARIST
Hymn at Exposition

1. O sa - lu - ta - ris Ho - sti - a
2. U - ni tri - no - que Do - mi - no

Quae coe - li pan - dis o - sti - um,
Sit sem - pi - ter - na glo - ri - a,

Bel - la pre - munt ho - sti - li - a,
Qui vi - tam si - ne ter - mi - no

Da ro - bur, fer au - xi - li - um.
No - bis do - net in pa - tri - a. A - men.

Hymn at Exposition

1. O sa - lu - ta - ris Ho - sti - a Quae
2. U - ni tri - no - que Do - mi - no Sit

coe - li pan - dis o - sti - um,
sem - pi - ter - na glo - ri - a,

Bel - la pre - munt ho - sti - li - a, Da
Qui vi - tam si - ne ter - mi - no No -

ro - bur, fer au - xi - li - um.
bis do - net in pa - tri - a. A - men.

HOLY EUCHARIST
Hymn at Exposition

1. O sa - lu - ta - ris Ho - sti - a Quae
2. U - ni tri - no - que Do - mi - no Sit

coe - li pan - dis o - sti - um,
sem - pi - ter - na glo - ri - a,

Bel - la pre - munt ho - sti - li - a, Da
Qui vi - tam si - ne ter - mi - no No -

ro - bur, fer au - xi - li - um.
bis do - net in pa - tri - a.

A - men.

Hymn at Exposition

1. O sa - lu - ta - ris Ho - sti -
2. U - ni tri - no - que Do - mi -

a Quae coe - li pan - dis o - sti - um,
no Sit sem - pi - ter - na glo - ri - a,

Bel - la pre - munt ho - sti - li - a, Da
Qui vi - tam si - ne ter - mi - no No -

ro - bur, fer au - xi - li - um.
bis do - net in pa - tri - a.

A-men.

HOLY EUCHARIST
Hymn at Exposition

1. O sa - lu - ta - ris Ho - sti - a
2. U - ni tri - no - que Do - mi - no

Quae coe - li pan - dis o - sti - um,____
Sit sem - pi - ter - na glo - ri - a,____

Bel - la pre - munt ho - sti - li - a,____
Qui vi - tam si - ne ter - mi - no____

·Da ro - bur, fer au - xi - li - um.____
No - bis do - net in pa - tri - a.____ A-men.

Hymn at Exposition

1. O sa - lu - ta - ris Ho - sti - a
2. U - ni tri - no - que Do - mi - no

Quae coe - li pan - dis o - sti - um,
Sit sem - pi - ter - na glo - ri - a,

Bel - la pre - munt ho - sti - li - a,____
Qui vi - tam si - ne ter - mi - no____

Da ro - bur, fer au - xi - li - um.
No - bis do - net in pa - tri - a. A - men.

Tune from Arundel Hymns by permission.

HOLY EUCHARIST
Hymn at Exposition

111

1. O sa - lu - ta - ris Ho - sti - a
2. U - ni tri - no - que Do - mi - no

Quae coe - li pan - dis o - sti - um,
Sit sem - pi - ter - na glo - ri - a,

Bel - la pre - munt ho - sti - li - a,
Qui vi - tam si - ne ter - mi - no

Da ro - bur, fer au - xi - li - um.
No - bis do - net in pa - tri - a. A - men.

Hymn at Exposition

1. O sa - lu - ta - ris Ho - sti - a Quae
2. U - ni tri - no - que Do - mi - no Sit

coe - li pan - dis o - sti - um, Bel - la pre - munt ho -
sem - pi - ter - na glo - ri - a, Qui vi - tam si - ne

sti - li - a, Da ro - bur, fer au - xi - li - um. A - men.
ter - mi - no No - bis do - net in pa - tri - a.

Tune from Arundel Hymns by permission.

HOLY EUCHARIST
Hymn for Procession

1. Pan - ge lin - gua glo - ri - o - si
2. No - bis da - tus, no - bis na - tus
3. In su - pre - mae noc - te coe - nae

Cor - po - ris my - ste - ri - um,
Ex in - tac - ta vir - gi - ne,
Re - cum - bens cum fra - tri - bus,

San - gui - ni - sque pre - ti - o - si,
Et in mun - do con - ver - sa - tus,
Ob - ser - va - ta le - ge ple - ne

Quem in mun - di pre - ti - um
Spar - so ver - bi se - mi - ne,
Ci - bis in le - ga - li - bus,

Fruc - tus   ven - tris   ge - ne - ro - si
Su - i   mo - ras   in - co - la - tus
Ci - bum   tur - bae   du - o - de - nae

Rex   ef - fu - dit   gen - ti - um.
Mi - ro   clau - sit   or - di - ne.   A - men.
Se   dat   su - is   ma - ni - bus.

:. Verbum caro, panem verum
   Verbo carnem efficit,
   Fitque sanguis Christi merum;
   Et si sensus deficit,
   Ad firmandum cor sincerum
   Sola fides sufficit.

5. Tantum ergo Sacramentum
   Veneremur cernui,
   Et antiquum documentum
   Novo cedat ritui.
   Praestet fides supplementum
   Sensuum defectui.

6. Genitori Genitoque
   Laus et jubilatio,
   Salus, honor, virtus quoque
   Sit et benedictio.
   Procedenti ab utroque
   Compar sit laudatio.

1. Tan-tum er - go— Sa-·cra-men - tum Ve - ne - re- mur

cer - nu - i,— Et an - ti -quum do - cu - men - tum

No - vo ce-dat ri - tu - i:— Prae-stet fi - des

sup - ple - men - tum Sen - su - um de - fec - tu - i.

2. Ge - ni - to - ri — Ge - ni - to - que Laus et ju -
bi - la - ti - o, — Sa - lus, ho - nor, vir - tus quo - que,
Sit et be - ne - dic - ti - o: Pro - ce - den - ti — ab
u - tro - que Com - par sit lau - da - ti - o. A - men.

HOLY EUCHARIST
Hymn before Benediction

1. Tan-tum er-go Sa-cra-men-tum Ve-ne-re-mur
2. Ge-ni-to-ri Ge-ni-to-que Laus et ju-bi-

cer-nu-i, Et an-ti-quum do-cu-men-tum
la-ti-o, Sa-lus, ho-nor, vir-tus quo-que,

No-vo ce-dat 'ri-tu-i: Prae-stet fi-des
Sit et be-ne-dic-ti-o: Pro-ce-den-ti

sup-ple-men-tum Sen-su-um de-fec-tu-i.
ab u-tro-que Com-par sit lau-da-ti-o. A-men.

1.Tan-tum er-go Sa-cra-men-tum Ve-ne-re-mur
2. Ge-ni-to-ri Ge-ni-to-que Laus et ju-bi-

cer-nu-i, Et an-ti-quum do-cu-men-tum
la-ti-o, Sa-lus, ho-nor, vir-tus quo-que,

No-vo ce-dat ri-tu-i: Prae-stet fi-des
Sit et be-ne-dic-ti-o: Pro-ce-den-ti

sup-ple-men-tum Sen-su-um de-fec-tu-i.
ab u-tro-que Com-par sit lau-da-ti-o. A-men.

HOLY EUCHARIST
Hymn before Benediction

1. Tan - tum er - go Sa - cra - men - tum Ve - ne - re - mur
2. Ge - ni - to - ri Ge - ni - to - que Laus et ju - bi -

cer - nu - i, Et an - ti - quum do - cu - men - tum
la - ti - o, Sa - lus, ho - nor, vir - tus quo - que,

No - vo ce - dat ri - tu - i: Prae - stet fi - des
Sit et be - ne - dic - ti - o: Pro - ce - den - ti

sup - ple - men - tum Sen - su - um de - fec - tu - i.
ab u - tro - que Com - par sit lau - da - ti - o. A-men.

Hymn before Benediction

1. Tan - tum er - go Sa - cra - men - tum Ve - ne - re - mur
2. Ge - ni - to - ri Ge - ni - to - que Laus et ju - bi -

cer - nu - i, Et an - ti - quum do - cu - men - tum
la - ti - o, Sa - lus, ho - nor, vir - tus quo - que,

No - vo ce - dat ri - tu - i: Prae - stet fi - des
Sit et be - ne - dic - ti - o: Pro - ce - den - ti

sup - ple - men - tum Sen - su - um de - fec - tu - i.
ab u - tro - que Com - par sit lau - da - ti - o. A - men.

HOLY EUCHARIST
Hymn before Benediction

1. Tan - tum er - go Sa - cra - men - tum
2. Ge - ni - to - ri Ge - ni - to - que

Ve - ne - re - mur cer - nu - i,
Laus et ju - bi - la - ti - o,

Et an - ti - quum do - cu - men - tum
Sa - lus, ho - nor, vir - tus quo - que,

No - vo ce - dat ri - tu - i:
Sit et be - ne - dic - ti - o:

Prae - stet fi - des sup - ple - men - tum
Pro - ce - den - ti ab u - tro - que

Sen - su - um de - fec - tu - i,
Com - par sit lau - da - ti - o,

Prae - stet fi - des sup - ple - men - tum
Pro - ce - den - ti ab u - tro - que

Sen - su - um de - fec - tu - i.
Com - par sit lau - da - ti - o. A - men.

120   HOLY EUCHARIST

Hymn before Benediction

No - vo___ ce - dat ri - tu - i:
Sit et___ be - ne - dic - ti - o:

Prae - stet fi - des sup - ple - men - tum
Pro - ce - den - ti ab u - tro - que

Sen - su - um de - fec - tu - i. A-men.
Com - par sit lau - da - ti - o.

121 HOLY EUCHARIST
Hymn before Benediction

1. Tan - tum er - go Sa - cra - men - tum
2. Ge - ni - to - ri Ge - ni - to - que

Ve - ne - re - mur cer - nu - i,
Laus et ju - bi - la - ti - o,

Et an - ti - quum do - cu - men - tum
Sa - lus, ho - nor, vir - tus quo - que,

No - vo ce - dat ri - tu - i:
Sit et be - ne - dic - ti - o:

HOLY EUCHARIST
Ascriptions of Praise after Benediction

Bles - sed be God. Bles - sed be His Ho - ly Name.

Bles - sed be Je - sus Christ true God and true Man.

Bles - sed be the Name of Je - sus.

Bles - sed be His Most Sa - cred Heart.

Bles-sed be Je-sus in the Most Ho-ly Sa-cra-ment of the Al - 'tar.

Bles-sed be the great Mo-ther of God, Ma - ry most ho - ly.

Bles-sed be her ho - ly and Im-ma-cu - late Con - cep - tion.

Bles-sed be the Name of Ma - ry Vir - gin and Mo-ther.

Bles - sed be God in His An-gels and in His Saints.

(122 - 2)

HOLY EUCHARIST
Psalm after Reposition

A - do - re - mus in ae - ter - - num

San - ctis - si - mum Sa - cra - men - tum.

Lau - da - te Do - mi - num o - mnes gen - tes,

lau - da - te e - um o - mnes po - pu - li,

Quo - ni - am con - fir - ma - ta est su - per nos mi - se - ri - cor - di -

a e - jus, et ve - ri - tas Do - mi - ni ma - net in ae - ter - num.

Repeat Adoremus etc.

Glo - ri - a Pa - tri et Fi - li - o, et Spi - ri - tu - i San - cto,

Si - cut e - rat in prin - ci - pi - o et nunc et sem - per,

Et in sae - cu - la sae - cu - lo - rum. A - men.

Repeat Adoremus etc.

SACRED HEART OF JESUS
Auctor beate saeculi

1. Blest Au - thor of the world, Re - deem - er
2. 'Twas Love that bade Thee take Our frame of
3. Thy Love that build - ed fair The earth, the

of our___ race, Thou ve - ry God of
mor - tal___ clay, New Ad - am, and bring
sea, the___ stars, That pit - ied old - en

rall

God, Light of the Fa - ther's face: A - men.
back What Ad - am bore a - way:
faults And brake our pris - on bars.

4. O may Thy Heart retain
For ay such wondrous Love.
Let all approach the Fount
And Thy sweet mercy prove.

5. For this alone the lance
Set free its saving flood,
To wash our sins away
In water and in Blood.

6. To Father, and to Son
And Holy Spirit, be
The kingdom and the power
Through all eternity.

SACRED HEART OF JESUS
Auctor beate saeculi

1. Blest Au-thor of the world, Re-deem-er of our
2. 'Twas Love that bade Thee take Our frame of mor-tal
3. Thy Love that build-ed fair The earth, the sea, the

race, Thou ve-ry God of God, Light
clay, New Ad-am, and bring back What
stars, That pit-ied old-en faults And

of the Fa-ther's face:
Ad-am bore a-way: A-men.
brake our pris-on bars.

Tune reprinted by permission of the Missionary Society of St. Paul the Apostle of the State of New York.

4. O may Thy Heart retain
   For ay such wondrous Love.
   Let all approach the Fount
   And Thy sweet mercy prove.

5. For this alone the lance
   Set free its saving flood,
   To wash our sins away
   In water and in Blood.

6. To Father, and to Son
   And Holy Spirit, be
   The kingdom and the power
   Through all eternity.

SACRED HEART OF JESUS

Auctor beate saeculi

1. O Christ, the world's Cre - a - tor bright, Who
2. Thy love com - pelled Thee to as - sume A
3. That love which once cre - a - ted all, The

didst man - kind from sin re - deem,
mor - tal Bo - dy, man to save;
earth, the stars, the won - drous sea,

The Fa - ther's ev - er glo - rious Light, True
Re - ver - sing ol - den Ad - am's doom, The
Took pi - ty on our pa - rents' fall, Broke

God of God, in bliss su - preme:
New - er Ad - am ran - som gave. A - men.
all our bonds and set us free.

Tune from Arundel Hymns by permission.

4. O Saviour, let Thy potent love
Flow ever from Thy bounteous Heart;
To nations that pure fount above
The grace of pardon will impart.

5. Thy Heart for this was opened wide,
And wounded by the soldier's spear,
That freely from Thy sacred side
Might flow the streams our souls to clear.

6. To God the Father, to the Son
And to the Holy Ghost the same,
Be glory, power, while ages run,
And endless rule in endless fame.

1. O Christ, the world's Cre - a - tor bright,
2. Thy love com - pelled Thee to as - sume
3. That love which once cre - a - ted all,

Who didst man - kind from sin re - deem,
A mor - tal Bo - dy, man to save;
The earth, the stars, the won - drous sea,

The Fa - ther's ev - er glo - rious Light,
Re - ver - sing ol - den Ad - am's doom,
Took pi - ty on our pa - rents' fall,

True God of God, in bliss su - preme:
The New - er Ad - am ran - som gave. A - men.
Broke all our bonds and set us free.

4. O Saviour, let Thy potent love
   Flow ever from Thy bounteous Heart;
   To nations that pure fount above
   The grace of pardon will impart.

5. Thy Heart for this was opened wide,
   And wounded by the soldier's spear,
   That freely from Thy sacred side
   Might flow the streams our souls to clear.

6. To God the Father, to the Son
   And to the Holy Ghost the same,
   Be glory, power, while ages run,
   And endless rule in endless fame.

SACRED HEART OF JESUS
En ut superba criminum

1. With what a cru - el dart The haugh-ty hosts of sin
2. The sol-dier poised the spear, 'Twas sin that shaped the aim:
3. From Je - sus' riv - en side The Church is born; a - gain

Have torn the Sav-iour's Heart, That love a - lone should win!
Its steel grew keen and clear On whet-stone of our shame.
Sal - va - tion's Ark swings wide Its por - tals un - to men.

Have torn the Sav-iour's Heart, That love a - lone should win!
Its steel grew keen and clear On whetstone of our shame. Amen.
Sal - va-tion's Ark swings wide Its por-tals un - to men.

4. And mercy, from within,
Doth pour a sevenfold flood,
To wash our robes of sin
In God's atoning Blood.

5. O shame if we return
To sins that wound Him so:
Our hearts should rather learn
Such love as His can show.

6. To Father, and to Son
And Holy Spirit, be
An equal honor done
Through all eternity.

En ut superba criminum

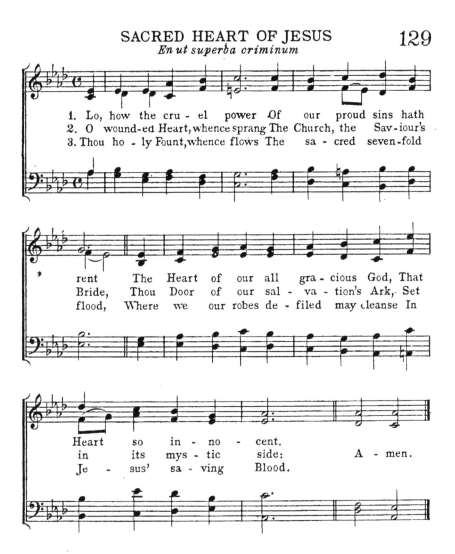

1. Lo, how the cru - el power Of our proud sins hath
2. O wound-ed Heart, whence sprang The Church, the Sav-iour's
3. Thou ho - ly Fount, whence flows The sa - cred seven-fold

rent The Heart of our all gra - cious God, That
Bride, Thou Door of our sal - va - tion's Ark, Set
flood, Where we our robes de - filed may cleanse In

Heart so in - no - cent.
in its mys - tic side: A - men.
Je - sus' sa - ving Blood.

4. By sorrowful relapse
   Thee we will rend no more,
   But like Thy flames, those types of love,
   Strive heavenward to soar.

5. Father and Son supreme,
   And Spirit, hear our cry,
   To Whom be glory, praise and power,
   Through all eternity.

130 SACRED HEART OF JESUS

Cor arca legem continens

1. O Heart, the Ark of Co - ve - nant, That nev - er-
2. O veil and tem - ple, ho - ly grail Of God's New
3. O ten - der Heart, all woun - ded thus That mor - tal

more a law shall hold Of fear and bon - dage,
Tes - ta - ment of love: O Veil, O Tem - ple,
eyes might find in Thee A mir - ror of that

as of old, But laws that peace and par - don grant:
far a - bove The tem - ple old, the riv - en veil. A - men.
cha - ri - ty Un - seen, but woun - ded still for us.

Tune from Catholic Church Hymnal by permission of J. Fischer & Bro.

4. O Symbol, speaking to our eyes
The altared Love, where He our Priest
Hath spread for us a twofold feast,
Bloody and bloodless Sacrifice.

5. Who would not love that loving Breast?
What ransomed soul can utter Nay
Nor choose to make that Heart for ay
The tabernacle of his rest?

SACRED HEART OF JESUS

Cor arca legem continens

1. O Christ, be - hind Thy tem - ple's veil, En -
2. But in Thy Bo - dy's Tem - ple new, Thy
3. And when that Heart in death__ was stilled, Each

closed in ark__ of gold, __ On stones en - gra - ven,
Life - Blood's throb-bing Shrine__ On flesh - ly ta - bles
tem - ple's veil was riven,__ And lo, with - in Thy

lay__ the law Thy fin - ger wrote of old.__
gra - ven held The law of love di - vine.__ A-men.
love's red shrine To us__ to look was given.__

4. There make us gaze, and see the love
Which drew Thee, for our sake,
O great High-Priest, Thyself to God
A Sacrifice to make.

5. Thou, Saviour, cause that every soul
Which Thou hast loved so well
May will within Thine opened Heart
In life and death to dwell.

6. O grant it, Father, only Son
And Spirit, God of grace,
To Whom all worship shall be done
In every time and place.

SACRED HEART OF JESUS

Cor arca legem continens

1. O ten - der Heart, strong Ark which doth en - shrine
2. O Heart, O Sanc - tu - a - ry un - de - filed,
3. Un - der love's sym - bol, sweet to us and dread,

The whole sweet law that rules the heart of man;
Of that new law of love un - to us given:
Mys - tic and hu - man woes hath Christ en - dured,

No lon - ger held as slaves be-neath a ban,
O Veil more pre - cious than of old was riven:
Our Priest Whose sa - cri - fice our Heaven se - cured,

Grate - ful and free we live by love di - vine,
O Tem - ple ho - lier than the an - cients piled,
Offe - ring His Blood and Flesh as wine and bread,

Grate - ful and free we live by love di - vine.
O Tem-ple ho - lier than the an-cients piled. A-men.
Offe - ring His Blood and Flesh as wine and bread.

4. What living heart is there that will not come
   At His redeeming call, that doth not sigh
   To give Him love for love, and will not fly
   Into His Heart, our everlasting home?

5. Honor be to the Father and the Son,
   And to the Holy Spirit honor be.
   All power, glory, sway, is of the Three
   Who through all ages live and love in one.

(132 - 2)

SACRED HEART OF JESUS
Quicumque certum quaeritis

1. All ye who seek a com-fort sure In
2. When Je-sus gave Him-self for you Up-
3. To sad and con-trite hearts what joy To

trou-ble and dis-tress, What-ev-er sor-row
on the Cross to die, For you was pierced His
hear those words so blest, 'All ye that la-bor,

vex the mind Or guilt the soul op-press:
Sa-cred Heart. O to that Heart draw nigh. A-men.
come to Me And I will give you rest!

4. What meeker than the Saviour's Heart
As on the Cross He lay?
It did His murderers forgive
And for their pardon pray.

5. O Heart, Thou Joy of Saints on high,
Thou hope of sinners here,
Attracted by those loving words,
To Thee I lift my prayer.

6. Wash Thou my wounds in that dear Blood
Which forth from Thee doth flow:
New grace, new hope inspire, a new
And better heart bestow.

Cor meum tibi dedo

1. O dear-est Love di - vine, My heart to Thee I give,
2. Who can re-quite the love That marks the won-drous plan
3. Thy Heart is o - pened wide, That, free - ly en-tering in,

Ex - chan-ging it for Thine, That Thou in me mayst live.
Where - by the God a - bove For me be-came a Man?
I may Thy guest a - bide And new-er life be - gin.

Most lov - ing and most meek, Hearts on - ly dost Thou seek: O
Thou sayst 'Give Me thy heart.' With it I free - ly part, In
This do - est Thou to gain My love and e'er re - tain: O

may my heart but prove A love like Thine, sweet Love.
hope that it may prove A love like Thine, sweet Love. Amen.
may my an - swer prove A love like Thine, sweet Love.

SACRED HEART OF JESUS
Summi Parentis Filio

1. O sole - be - got - ten Son, Fa -
2. Thou, Who with - in Thy breast The
3. O Vic - tim of our sin: Who

ther of world to be, O Prince of Peace, to
wound of love didst bear, Mak'st them the pain to
bade the lance make wide The por - tals that would

Thee Our praise be done.
share Who love Thee best. A - men.
hide The wound with - in?

4. O wondrous Fount of Love:
   O panting hart's desire:
   O sin-consuming Fire
   Allumed above!

5. Within Thy Heart, dear Lord,
   Our trembling spirits place:
   Grant us abundant grace
   And Heaven's reward.

6. To Jesus, Mary's Son,
   Father and Paraclete,
   Let endless honor meet
   And praise be done.

Summi Parentis Filio

1. To Christ the Prince of Peace, And
2. Deep in His Heart for us The
3. O Je - sus, Vic - tim blest, What

Son of God most high, The Fa - ther of the
wound of love He bore, That love where-with He
else but love di - vine Could Thee con - strain to

world to come, Our joy - ful praise we cry.
still in - flames The hearts that Him a - dore. A-men.
o - pen thus That Sa - cred Heart of Thine.

Tune from Catholic Church Hymnal by permission of J. Fischer & Bro.

4. O Fount of endless life:
O Spring of waters clear:
O Flame celestial cleansing all
Who unto Thee draw near.

5. Hide me in Thy dear Heart,
For thither do I fly;
There seek Thy grace through life, in death
Thine immortality.

6. To God the Father praise,
Praise to th'Eternal Son,
And praise to God the Holy Ghost
While endless ages run.

137 SACRED HEART OF JESUS
Cor Jesu Cor purissimum

1. O Heart of Jesus, pu-rest Heart, A
2. Most hum-ble Heart of all that beat, Heart
3. But e-ven were my heart on fire With

Shrine of Ho-li-ness Thou art,
full of good-ness, meek and sweet,
all the Ser-a-phim's de-sire,

Cleanse Thou my heart, so sor-did, cold, And
Give me a heart more like to Thine, And
Till love a con-fla-gra-tion proved, Not

stained by sins so ma-ni-fold.
light the flame of love in mine. A-men.
yet wouldst Thou e-nough be loved.

4. That therefore Thou mayst worthily
   Be loved, O loving Lord, by me,
   That love wherewith Thy Heart doth burn
   Give me to love Thee in return.

Cor amore plenum

1. O Heart of Je - sus, Heart of God, O
2. The poo - rest, sad - dest heart on earth May
3. The ve - ry sound of those sweet words, 'The

source of bound - less love, By An - gels praised, by
claim Thee for its own, O bur - ning, throb - bing
Sa - cred Heart,' can give To lone - li - est of

Saints a - dored, From their bright thrones a - bove.
Heart of Christ, Too late, too lit - tle known. A - men.
bur - dened souls Strength to en - dure and live.

4. To Thee, O Jesus, thus I come,
   A poor and helpless child,
   And on Thy saying 'Come to Me'
   My only hope I build.

SACRED HEART OF JESUS

Dignare me O Jesu rogo te

1. My dear - est Sav - iour I would fain With -
2. In vain the de - mon lays his snares, In
3. And though the flesh wage war, my soul In

in Thy Sa - cred Heart re - main: O let me safe a -
vain the bribe of world - ly wares: He can not tempt a
guil - ty pleas-ures to con - trol, For me is o - pened

bide For - ev - er in Thy Woun-ded Side.
pride For - got - ten in Thy Woun-ded Side. A - men.
wide The por - tal of Thy Woun-ded Side.

4. When fading sight and fluttering breath
   Proclaim the near approach of death,
   O Saviour, let me hide
   And die within Thy Wounded Side.

Dignare me O Jesu rogo te

1. Je - sus, grant me this, I pray,
2. If the e - vil one pre - pare,
3. If the flesh, more dange - rous still,

Ev - er in Thy Heart to stay;
Or the world, a temp - ting snare,
Tempt my soul to deeds of ill,

Let me ev - er - more a - bide
I am safe when I a - bide
Naught I fear when I a - bide

Hid - den in Thy Woun - ded Side.
In Thy Heart and Woun - ded Side. A - men.
In Thy Heart and Woun - ded Side.

4. Death will come one day to me;
Jesus, cast me not from Thee;
Dying let me still abide
In Thy Heart and Wounded Side.

SACRED HEART OF JESUS
Summi Regis Cor, aveto

1. Thee with joy - ful soul I hail, Heart of
2. By what love wert Thou o'er - come, By what
3. O how sharp the cru - el strife And Thy

Je - sus, heaven - ly King; Let Thy love for me a -
wring - ing grief and pain, E'en to sink with - in the
pangs up - on the Tree, Swee - test Heart, our home of

vail While my tongue Thy praise shall sing.
tomb, So from death our souls to gain. A - men.
life, When Thou gav'st Thy life for me.

4. By that Death upon the Rood,
   Loving Heart of Christ my King,
   Let me show my gratitude,
   Seek Thee, cleave to Thee and cling.

5. Tender Heart, with love afire,
   Wash my heart of sinful stain,
   Kindle thoughts of pure desire,
   Driving forth the vile and vain.

6. Be Thy love my living cure,
   Weak and sinful though I be;
   Thou canst make my healing sure,
   Wound my soul with love for Thee.

7. Heart of Jesus, open wide,
   Sweeter Thou than fragrant rose;
   Let my soul in Thee abide,
   There to soothe all pains and woes.

8. Let me live for love of Thee
   And forget Thee nevermore;
   Let Thy love my glory be
   Still to honor, praise, adore.

SACRED HEART OF JESUS

Fons totius consolationis

1. Dear Je - sus, Thou a ha - ven art From life's tem - pes - tuous sea; All find a ref - uge in Thy Heart Who turn in love to Thee.

2. Thy name falls sweet on ex - iles' ear As mu - sic from a - bove; It stays the mour - ner's anx - ious fear And tel - leth naught but love. A - men.

3. The bro - ken heart with hea - ling balm Thy change - less love doth fill; Thou say - est 'Peace,' the winds are calm And eve - ry wave is still.

4. O hope and joy of life's lone way,
   May Thy sweet peace arise,
   Which turns the night to blissful day
   And earth to Paradise.

5. Dear Jesus, when death's night shall fall,
   By all Thy love so blest,
   May longing exiles hear Thee call
   The weary to their rest.

1. Hail Je - sus, Who for my poor sake Sweet
2. To end - less a - ges let us praise The
3. O Blood that can from God im - plore His

Blood from Ma - ry's veins didst take And
Pre - cious Blood, whose price could raise The
gra - cious par - don and re - store The

shed it all for me, And shed it all for me.
world from wrath and sin, The world from wrath and sin.
Heaven which sin had lost, The Heaven which sin had lost.

O blessed be my Saviour's Blood,
My life, my light, my only good,
My life, my light, my only good
To all eternity.

Whose streams our inward thirst appease,
And heal the sinner's worst disease,
And heal the sinner's worst disease
If he but bathe therein.

While Abel's blood for vengeance pleads,
What Jesus shed still intercedes,
What Jesus shed still intercedes
For those who wrong Him most.

A-men.

4. To be but sprinkled from the wells
Of Jesus' Precious Blood excels
Earth's best and highest bliss.
The ministers of wrath divine
Hurt not the happy hearts that shine
With those red drops of His.

5. O there is joy amid the Saints
And hell's despairing courage faints
When this sweet song we raise.
Now louder, yes and louder still,
This earth with mighty chorus fill
The Precious Blood to praise.

(143-2)

1. Glo - ry be to Je - sus,
2. Grace and life e - ter - nal
3. Blest through end - less a - ges

Who in bit - ter pains Poured for me the
In that Blood I find; Blest he His com -
Be the pre - cious stream Which from end - less

life - Blood From His sa - cred Veins.
pas - sion In - fi - nite - ly kind. A-men.
tor - ment Doth the world re - deem.

4. There the fainting spirit
   Drinks of life her fill,
   There as in a fountain
   Laves herself at will.

5. Blood of Christ outflowing
   Soothes the Father's ire,
   Opes the gate of Heaven,
   Quells eternal fire.

6. Abel's blood for vengeance
   Pleaded to the skies,
   But the Blood of Jesus
   For our pardon cries.

7. Oft as it is sprinkled
   On our guilty hearts,
   Satan in confusion
   Terror-struck departs.

8. Oft as earth exulting
   Wafts its praise on high
   Hell with terror trembles,
   Heaven is filled with joy.

9. Lift ye then your voices,
   Swell the mighty flood,
   Louder still and louder
   Praise the Precious Blood.

1. Glo - ry be to Je - sus,
2. Grace and life e - ter - nal
3. Blest through end - less a - ges

Who in bit - ter pains Poured for me the
In that Blood I find; Blest he His com -
Be the pre - cious stream Which from end - less

life - Blood From His sa - cred Veins.
pas - sion In - fi - nite - ly kind. A-men.
tor - ment Doth the world re - deem.

4. There the fainting spirit
Drinks of life her fill,
There as in a fountain
Laves herself at will.

5. Blood of Christ outflowing
Soothes the Father's ire,
Opes the gate of Heaven,
Quells eternal fire.

6. Abel's blood for vengeance
Pleaded to the skies,
But the Blood of Jesus
For our pardon cries.

7. Oft as it is sprinkled
On our guilty hearts,
Satan in confusion
Terror-struck departs.

8. Oft as earth exulting
Wafts its praise on high,
Hell with terror trembles,
Heaven is filled with joy.

9. Lift ye then your voices,
Swell the mighty flood,
Louder still and louder
Praise the Precious Blood.

146 PRECIOUS BLOOD
Ira justa Conditoris

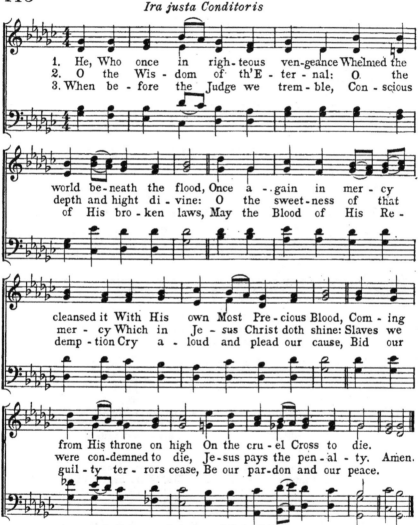

1. He, Who once in righ-teous ven-geance Whelmed the world be-neath the flood, Once a-gain in mer-cy cleansed it With His own Most Pre-cious Blood, Com-ing from His throne on high On the cru-el Cross to die.

2. O the Wis-dom of th'E-ter-nal: O the depth and hight di-vine: O the sweet-ness of that mer-cy Which in Je-sus Christ doth shine: Slaves we were con-demned to die, Je-sus pays the pen-al-ty. Amen.

3. When be-fore the Judge we trem-ble, Con-scious of His bro-ken laws, May the Blood of His Re-demp-tion Cry a-loud and plead our cause, Bid our guil-ty ter-rors cease, Be our par-don and our peace.

By permission of 4. Prince and Author of Salvation, *Novello & Co. Ltd.*
Lord of Majesty supreme,
Jesus, praise to Thee be given
By the world Thou didst redeem:
To the Father glory be
And the Spirit One with Thee.

Salvete Christi vulnera

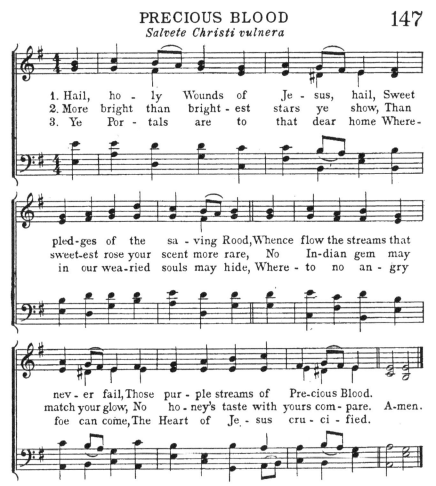

1. Hail, ho - ly Wounds of Je - sus, hail, Sweet pled-ges of the sa - ving Rood, Whence flow the streams that nev - er fail, Those pur - ple streams of Pre-cious Blood.

2. More bright than bright - est stars ye show, Than sweet-est rose your scent more rare, No In-dian gem may match your glow, No ho - ney's taste with yours com - pare. A-men.

3. Ye Por - tals are to that dear home Where- in our wea-ried souls may hide, Where - to no an - gry foe can come, The Heart of Je - sus cru - ci - fied.

4. In full atonement of our guilt,
Not sparing self, the Saviour trod,
E'en till His Heart's best Blood was spilt,
The wine-press of the wrath of God.

5. Come, bathe you in that healing flood,
All ye who mourn, by sin oppressed;
Your only hope is Jesus' Blood,
His Sacred Heart your only rest.

6. All praise to Him, th' Eternal Son,
At God's right hand enthroned above,
Whose Blood our full redemption won,
Whose Spirit seals the gift of love.

BLESSED VIRGIN MARY
Quem terra, pontus, sidera

1. The God Whom earth and sea and sky
2. The God Whose will by . moon and sun
3. How blest that Mo - ther, in whose shrine

A - dore and laud and mag - ni - fy,
And all things in due course is done,
The world's Cre - a - tor, Lord di - vine,

Who o'er their three - fold fab - ric reigns, The
Is borne up - on a Mai - den's breast By
Whose hand con - tains the earth and sky, Vouch -

Vir - gin's fault - less form con - tains.
ful - lest heaven - ly grace pos - sessed. A - men.
safed as in His Ark to lie.

4. How blest in words by Gabriel brought,
How blest by work the Spirit wrought,
From whom the great Desire of Earth
Took human flesh and human birth.

5. All honor, laud and glory be,
O Jesus, Virgin - born, to Thee;
Be glory also as is meet
To Father and to Paraclete.

Ave maris stella

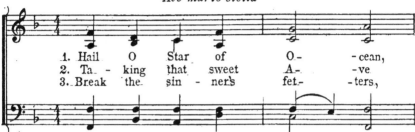

1. Hail O Star of O- -cean,
2. Ta- king that sweet A- -ve
3. Break the sin - ner's fet- -ters,

God's own Mo - ther blest,____ Ev - er sin -less
Which from Ga - briel came,____ Peace con -firm with -
Make our blind-ness day,____ Chase all e - vil

Vir - gin, Gate of Heaven-ly Rest.
in us, Changing E - va's name. A - men.
from us, For all bles -sings pray.

4. Show thyself a Mother,
   May the Word Divine,
   Born for us thine Infant,
   Hear our prayers through thine.

5. Virgin all excelling,
   Mildest of the mild,
   Free from guilt preserve us,
   Meek and undefiled.

6. Keep our life all spotless,
   Make our way secure,
   Till we find in Jesus
   Joy for evermore.

7. Praise to God the Father,
   Honor to the Son,
   In the Holy Spirit
   Be the glory one.

Tune from Arundel Hymns by permission.

150 BLESSED VIRGIN MARY

Ave maris stella

1. Hail O - cean's beau - teous Star, Hail
2. Es - ta - blish us in peace; Re -
3. A Mo - ther show thy - self, Us

God's own Mo - ther blest, Hail ev - er Vir - gin
ver - sing E - va's name, Let Ga - briel's A - ve
chil - dren make thy care, To Him Who thine be -

Queen, Hail Gate of Heaven - ly Rest.
be For us a tru - er claim. A - men.
came For us con - vey our prayer.

4. Things evil drive away,
Unloose the captive's chain,
Bring light unto the blind,
All needed favors gain.

5. O pure, O spotless Maid,
Whose virtues all excel,
O make us chaste and mild
And all our passions quell.

6. Preserve our lives unstained
And guard us on our way,
Until with thee be ours
The joys that ne'er decay.

7. To God the Father praise,
With Christ His only Son,
And to the Holy Ghost,
Thrice - blessed Three in One.

O gloriosa virginum

1. O glo - rious Vir - gin, throned on high A - bove the
2. Through thy dear Off-spring we re - ceive The bliss once
3. Thou art the Door of Heaven's high King, Of Light the

star - il - lu - mined sky, There-to or - dained, thy per - son
lost through hap - less Eve, And Heav'n to mor - tals o - pen
path - way glis - te - ning. Ye ran-somed na-tions, hail to

lent To thy Cre - a - tor nou - rish-ment.
lies, Now thou art Por - tal of the skies. A-men.
Heaven Our Life-Spring through a Vir - gin given.

4. All honor, laud and glory, be
   O Jesus Virgin - born to Thee,
   All glory ever as is meet
   To Father and to Paraclete.

Gratia plena

1. Hail Ma - ry, Pearl of Grace, Pure flower of Ad - am's
2. Thou Queen of high es - tate, Con - ceived Im - ma - cu -
3. A fai - rer, pu - rer Eve, Didst thou her fall re -

race, And ves - sel rare of God's e - lec - tion;
late To form In - car - nate Love's pure dwel - ling:
trieve, For man's debt giv - ing God in pay - ment:

Un - stained as vir - gin snow, Se - rene as sun - set
The Spi - rit found His rest With - in thy sin - less
Thy spot - less feet are pressed Up - on the ser - pent's

glow, We sin - ners crave thy sure pro - tec - tion.
breast, And hence flow joys be - yond all tel - ling. A - men.
crest, God's stars thy crown, His sun thy rai - ment.

Tune from   4. Through His dear Blood Who died,   *Westminster Hymnal.*
By sinners crucified,
Art thou preserved, and we forgiven.
Help us to conquer sin,
That we may enter in,
Through thee, the golden Gate, to Heaven.

Gratia plena

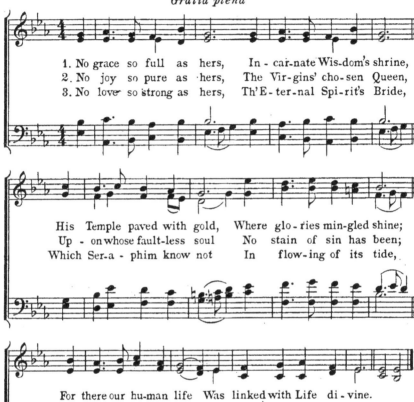

1. No grace so full as hers, In-car-nate Wis-dom's shrine,
2. No joy so pure as hers, The Vir-gins' cho-sen Queen,
3. No love so strong as hers, Th'E-ter-nal Spi-rit's Bride,

His Temple paved with gold, Where glo-ries min-gled shine;
Up - on whose fault-less soul No stain of sin has been;
Which Ser-a - phim know not In flow-ing of its tide,

For there our hu-man life Was linked with Life di - vine.
The pu-rest joy by far That high-est Heaven has seen. Amen.
Where reign-ing with the King She nev - er leaves His side.

Tune from Arundel Hymns by permission.

4. No peace so deep as hers
  Who reigns among the blest,
  Where sorrow comes no more,
  Where weary souls find rest;
  Of peaceful realms the Queen
  On Sion's highest crest. .

5. No light so sweet as hers,
  The crown of pure desires,
  Where glory dazzles not,
  Where sweetness never tires,
  Above the Saints redeemed,
  Above the Angel choirs.

BLESSED VIRGIN MARY
Immaculate Conception

1. Ma - ry Im - ma - cu - late, Star of the Mor - ning, Cho - sen be - fore the cre - a - tion be - gan,____
2. Here, in an or - bit of sha - dow and sad - ness, Veil - ing thy splen - dor, thy course thou hast run;____
3. Sin - ners, we wor - ship thy sin - less per - fec - tion; Fal - len and weak, for thy pi - ty we plead;____

From Rev. S. Gregory Ould's Book of Hymns by permission.

. Cho - sen to bring, in the
Now thou art throned in all
Grant us the shield of thy

light of thy daw - ning, Woe to the
glo - ry and glad - ness, Crowned by the
sove - reign pro - tec - tion; Mea - sure thine

ser - pent and res - cue to man:
hand of thy Sa - viour and Son. A - men.
aid by the depth of our need.

4. Frail is our nature and strict our probation;
   Watchful the foe that would lure us to wrong;
   Succor our souls in the hour of temptation,
   Mary Immaculate, tender and strong.

5. See how the wiles of the serpent assail us,
   See how we waver and flinch in the fight:
   Let thine immaculate merit avail us,
   Make of our weakness a proof of thy might.

6. Bend from thy throne at the note of our crying,
   Bend to this earth which thy footsteps have trod:
   Stretch out thine arms to us living and dying,
   Mary Immaculate, Mother of God.

(154- 2)

BLESSED VIRGIN MARY
Immaculate Conception

1. O pu - rest of crea - tures, sweet
2. Deep night hath come down on this
3. The Church doth what God had first

Mo - ther, sweet Maid, The one spot - less
rough - spo - ken world; The ban - ners of
taught her to do; He looked o'er the

shrine where - in Je - sus was laid,
dark - ness are bold - ly un - furled;
world to find hearts that were true;

Tune from Joseph Groiss, op. 29, 12 German Hymns in honor of St. Mary, with permission of L. Schwann, publisher, Düsseldorf, Germany.

Dark night hath come down on us,
The tem - pest - tossed Church, all her
Through a - ges He looked and He

Mo - ther, and we Look out for thy
eyes are on thee, They look to thy
found none but thee: He loved thy clear

shi - ning, sweet Star of the Sea.
shi - ning, sweet Star of the Sea. A - men.
shi - ning, sweet Star of the Sea.

4. He gazed on thy soul: it was spotless and fair,
   The trail of the serpent had never been there.
   None ever had owned thee, dear Mother, but He:
   He blest thy clear shining, sweet Star of the Sea.

5. Earth gave Him one lodging; 'twas deep in thy breast:
   And God found a home where the sinner finds rest.
   His home and His hiding-place both were in thee;
   He joyed in thy shining, sweet Star of the Sea.

6. O blissful and calm was the wonderful rest
   Thou gavest thy God in thy virginal breast.
   If Heaven He left He found heaven in thee;
   He shone in thy shining, sweet Star of the Sea.

BLESSED VIRGIN MARY
The Purification

1. O pu-ri-fy the first soft ray That lights the mor-ning
2. And pu-ri-fy the crys-tal drops That gem the vi-o-
3. Then pu-ri-fy with all your skill That light-some sno-wy

sky, And tints with gold the sno-wy clouds A-
let, And crown the ope-ning rose-bud's brow With
flake, The wa-ter-li-lies as they float Up-

long its path-way high; And pu-ri-fy the
dia-mond co-ro-net; The hy-a-cinth a-
on the sil-ver lake; The whi-test dove with

moon-beam fair That smiles o'er land and sea;
mid its leaves, The blos-som on the tree;
plumes fresh bathed, The pearls be-neath the sea;

For though their light is ve - ry pure 'Tis far less pure than
Though pure in na - ture's love - li - ness, Less pure are they than
For though they all are ve - ry pure, Less pure are they than

she: O far less pure than she who stood Be -
she: Less pure than she, that Vir - gin Blest, For
she, The Vir - gin - Mo - ther of our God With -

fore the tem - ple - gate, Her soul a fount of
who can es - ti - mate Her more than an - gel
out the tem - ple - gate: The Flower of Is - rael,

heaven - ly light, Ma - ry Im - ma - cu - late.
pu - ri - ty? Ma - ry Im - ma - cu - late. A - men.
snow - white Pearl, Ma - ry Im - ma - cu - late.

Tune from Arundel Hymns by permission.

(156 - 2)

BLESSED VIRGIN MARY
The Annunciation.

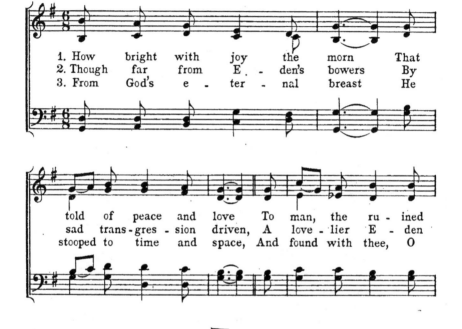

1. How bright with joy the morn That
2. Though far from E - den's bowers By
3. From God's e - ter - nal breast He

told of peace and love To man, the ru - ined
sad trans - gres - sion driven, A love - lier E - den
stooped to time and space, And found with thee, O

and for - lorn, De - scen - ding from a - bove.
shall be ours, For Christ came down from Heaven. A - men.
Mai - den blest, His low - ly dwel - ling - place.

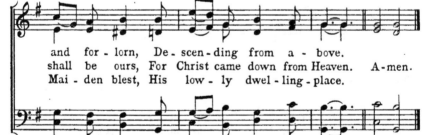

Tune reprinted by permission of the Missionary Society of St. Paul the Apostle of the State of New York.

4. And in the lowlier tomb
   He scornéd not to lie,
   That our frail mortal might assume
   His immortality.

5. Praise to the Virgin - born
   As to the Father be,
   Through endless life's unwaning morn,
   And Holy Ghost to Thee.

Praeclara custos virginum

1. O Guar - dian blest of vir - gin souls, Thou Gate of
2. Fair Li - ly found a - mid the thorns, Most beau - teous
3. Thou Tower a - gainst the dra - gon proof, Thou Star to

Bliss to man for-given, True Mo - ther of Al-migh - ty
Dove with wings of gold, Thou Rod whose ten - der root gave
storm- tossed voya-gers dear, Our course lies o'er a trea-cherous

God, Thou hope of earth and joy of Heaven.
forth That hea - ling Flower since long fore - told. A - men.
deep, Be thine the light by which we steer.

4. Dispel the mists that round us hang,
   Keep far the fatal shoals away,
   And while through darkling waves we sweep,
   Make clear a path to life and day.

5. O Jesus, born of Virgin bright,
   All praise and glory be to Thee,
   To God the Father infinite
   And Holy Ghost eternally.

BLESSED VIRGIN MARY
O stella Jacob fulgida

1. Star of Ja - cob, ev - er beam -ing With a ra - diance
2. All in stoles of snow- y white-ness Un - to thee the
3. Joy - ful in thy path they scat - ter Ros - es white and

all di - vine, Mid the stars of high-est Heav - en
An - gels sing, Un - to thee the vir - gin cho - rus,
lil - ies fair, Yet with thy sur - pass-ing beau - ty

Glows no pu - rer ray than thine.
Moth - er of th'E - ter - nal King. A - men.
Rose nor li - ly may com - pare.

4. O that this low earth of mortals,
Answering to th' angelic strain,
With thy praises might re - echo
Till the heavens replied again.

5. Honor, glory, virtue, merit
Be to Thee, O Virgin's Son,
With the Father and the Spirit,
While eternal ages run.

Virgo praedicanda

1. Vir - gin whol - ly mar - vel - lous,
2. Heaven and earth, and all that is,
3. Cher - u - bim with four - fold face

Who didst bear God's Son for us,
Thrilled to - day with ec - sta - sies,
Are no peers of thine in grace,

Worth - less is my tongue and weak
Chan - ting glo - ry un - to thee,
And the six - winged Ser - a - phim,

Of thy ho - li - ness to speak.
Sing thy praise with fes - tal glee. A - men.
Mid thy splen - dor, shine but dim.

4. Purer art thou than are all
   Heavenly Hosts angelical,
   Who delight with pomp and state
   On thy beauteous Child to wait.

BLESSED VIRGIN MARY

Causa nostrae laetitiae

1. Raise your voi - ces, vales and mountains, Flowe - ry mea - dows,
2. Murm'-ring brooks your trib - ute bring-ing, Lit - tle birds with
3. Say, sweet Vir - gin, we im-plore thee, Say what beau - ty

streams and foun - tains, Praise, O praise the love - liest Mai - den
joy - ful sing - ing, Come with mirth - ful prai - ses la - den:
God sheds o'er thee: Praise and thanks to Him be giv - en

The Cre - a - tor ev - er made.
To your Queen be hom - age paid. A - men.
Who in love cre - a - ted thee.

Tune from Arundel Hymns by permission.

4. Like a sun with splendor glowing
   Gleams thy heart with love o'erflowing;
   Like the moon in starry heaven
   Shines thy peerless purity.

5. Like the rose and lily blooming,
   Sweetly heaven and earth perfuming,
   Stainless, spotless, thou appearest:
   Queenly beauty graces thee.

6. But to God, in Whom thou livest,
   Sweeter joy and praise thou givest,
   When, to Him in beauty nearest,
   Yet so humble thou canst be.

Janua coeli

1. O Gate of end - less Bliss, Whose sweet ce - les - tial ray Comes shi - ning o'er the vast a - byss That sev - ers night from day:
2. My soul un - furls her wings To soar a - loft to thee, And far re - moved from earth - ly things A - dores thy Mys - te - ry. A-men.
3. The proph - et saw that Fane Of heaven - ly beau - ty fair, Where De - i - ty it - self would deign To find a dwel - ling there.

4. One Portal stood alone,
Of peerless pearl its frame;
There would the Lord ascend His throne
And Mary was its name.

5. All hail, thou matchless Maid:
An entrance make for me
Where He in glory is displayed
Who came to us through thee.

BLESSED VIRGIN MARY
Te Redemptoris Dominique nostri

1. Glo - rious Vir - gin, thee we sing, Mo - ther of our
2. Though the powers of e - vil rage And their fier - cest
3. Fu - ry's shaft shall harm - less be To the pure that

Lord and King, Lov - ing aid in all our woes,
bat - tles wage, Though the an - cient foe as - sail,
call on thee, Seek thy in - ter - ces - sion sweet,

Bring - ing sol - ace and re - pose.
'Gainst thy help shall naught pre - vail. A - men.
Ben - ding at thy bles - sed feet.

4. Thou hast saved us from the rod
By the strong right hand of God;
Yield us still thy tender care,
Shield us by thy powerful prayer.

5. To the glorious Trinity
Endless love and power shall be;
Heaven and earth Thy praise shall sing,
Everlasting God and King.

Hymn for Month of May

1. O Ma - ry, dea-rest Mo-ther, We greet thee once a - gain,
2. And so, O dea-rest Mo-ther, Be - fore the sim-ple shrine
3. Look down on us thy chil-dren, O Mo - ther dear, look down;

This month of all most wel-come To An-gels and to men;
Which we have decked with flow-ers Be - cause we call it thine,
The Mo-ther's face beams kind-ly When oth - er fa - ces frown.

The month of birds and blos-soms, The flowe-ry sun-ny May,
We kneel to of - fer fra-grance And prayer and song to thee.
So though thou'rt Queen of Hea - ven And reignst in joy a - bove,

When earth and sky, dear Mo - ther, To thee fond trib-ute pay.
Look down, O dea-rest Mo - ther, Look down to hear and see. Amen.
Yet still, O dea-rest Mo - ther, Look down on us with love.

4. In Heaven's eternal May-time,
Whose sunlight is the Lamb,
The gladness and the glory,
The rapture and the calm,
We'll praise thee and we'll bless thee
With happy Saints above,
If now, O mighty Mother,
Thou look on us with love.

BLESSED VIRGIN MARY
Hymn for Month of May

1. The leaves are green, the flowers are sweet, And rich the hues of
2. The grass is green, but wait a while, 'Twill grow and then will
3. The green, green grass, the glittering grove, The heaven's ma-jes-tic

May. We see them in the gar-dens fair And
wither. The flowe-rets, bright-ly as they smile, Shall
dome, They im-age forth a tende-rer bower, A

mar-ket pla-ces gay, And all a-long our
per-ish al-to-gether. The mer-ry sun, you
more re-ful-gent home. They tell us of that

roads and lanes, Out-spread to meet our eye,
sure would say It ne'er could set in gloom,
Pa-ra-dise Of ev-er-las-ting rest,

From Arundel Hymns by permission.

The ver - dant fields keep kind - ly pace With blue tran-spa-rent
But earth's best joys have all an end And sin a hea-vy
Of Sa - lem's Tree, all flowers and fruit, The sweet-est, yet the

sky. O Mo - ther - Maid, be thou our aid Now
doom. But, Mo - ther - Maid, thou dost not fade; With
best. O Ma - ry, pure and beau - ti - ful, Thou

in the ope - ning year, Lest sights of earth to
stars a - bove thy brow, The beau - teous moon be -
art the Queen of May: Our gar - lands wear a -

sin give birth And bring the temp - ter near.
neath thy feet, For ev - er throned art thou. A-men.
bout thy hair And ne'er will they de - cay.

BLESSED VIRGIN MARY
Hymn for Month of May

1. This is the im - age of the Queen Who
2. The hom - age of - fered at the feet Of
3. Full sweet the flowe - rets we have culled This

reigns in bliss a - bove; Of her who is the
Ma - ry's im - age here To Ma - ry's self at
im - age to a - dorn, But swee - ter far is

hope of men, Whom men and an - gels love.
once as - cends A - bove the star - ry sphere.
Ma - ry's self, That rose with - out a thorn.

Most ho - ly Ma - ry, at thy feet I
Most ho - ly Ma - ry, at thy feet I
Most ho - ly Ma - ry, at thy feet I

bend a sup-pliant knee: In this thine own sweet
bend a sup-pliant knee: In all my joy, in
bend a sup-pliant knee: When I on bed of

month of May, Dear Mo - ther of my
all my pain, O Vir - gin born with -
death shall lie, By Him Who did for

God, I pray Do thou re - mem - ber me. A - men.
out a stain, Do thou re - mem - ber me.
sin - ners die, Do thou re - mem - ber me.

Tune from Westminster Hymnal.

4. O Lady, by the stars that make
A glory round thy head,
And by thy pure uplifted hands
That for thy children plead,
When at the Judgment-seat I stand
And my Redeemer see,
When waves of night around me roll
And hell is raging for my soul,
O then remember me.

(166-2)

1. Sta - bat Ma - ter do - lo - ro - sa
2. O quam tri - stis et af - fli - cta
3. Quis est ho - mo qui non fle - ret,

Ju - xta cru - cem la - cri - mo - sa,
Fu - it il - la be - ne - di - cta
Ma - trem Chri - sti si vi - de - ret.

Dum pen - de - bat Fi - li - us.
Ma - ter U - ni - ge - ni - ti!
In tan - to sup - pli - ci - o?

Cu - jus a - ni - mam ge - men - tem,
Quae mae - re - bat et do - le - bat,
Quis non pos - set con - tri - sta - ri,

Tune from Arundel Hymns by permission

Con - tri - sta - tam et do - len - tem,
Pi - a Ma - ter, dum vi - de - bat
Chri - sti Ma - trem con - tem - pla - ri

Per - tran - si - vit gla - di - us.
Na - ti poe - nas in - cly - ti. A - men.
Do - len - tem cum Fi - li - o?

4. Pro peccatis suæ gentis
Vidit Jesum in tormentis,
Et flagellis subditum.
Vidit suum dulcem Natum
Moriendo desolatum,
Dum emisit spiritum.

5. Eia Mater, fons amoris,
Me sentire vim doloris
Fac, ut tecum lugeam.
Fac ut ardeat cor meum
In amando Christum Deum,
Ut sibi complaceam.

6. Sancta Mater, istud agas,
Crucifixi fige plagas
Cordi meo valide.
Tui. Nati vulnerati,
Tam dignati pro me pati,
Poenas mecum divide

7. Fac me tecum pie flere,
Crucifixo condolere,
Donec ego vixero.
Juxta Crucem tecum stare,
Et me tibi sociare
In planctu desidero.

8. Virgo virginum præclara,
Mihi jam non sis amara;
Fac me tecum plangere.
Fac ut portem Christi mortem,
Passionis fac consortem,
Et plagas recolere.

9. Fac me plagis vulnerari,
Fac me Cruce inebriari,
Et cruore Filii.
Flammis ne urar succensus,
Per te, Virgo, sim defensus
In die judicii.

10. Christe, cum sit hinc exire,
Da per Matrem me venire
Ad palmam victoriæ.
Quando corpus morietur,.
Fac ut animæ donetur
Paradisi gloria.

168 **BLESSED VIRGIN MARY**
Stabat Mater

1. At the Cross her station keeping,
2. O how sad and sore distressed
3. Who on Christ's dear Mother gazing

Stood the mournful Mother weeping,
Was that Mother, ever Blessed,
In her trouble so amazing,

Close to Jesus till the last.
Of the Sole-begotten One!
Born of woman, would not weep?

Through her heart, His sorrow sharing,
O that silent ceaseless mourning,
Who on Christ's dear Mother thinking,

Tune from Arundel Hymns by permission.

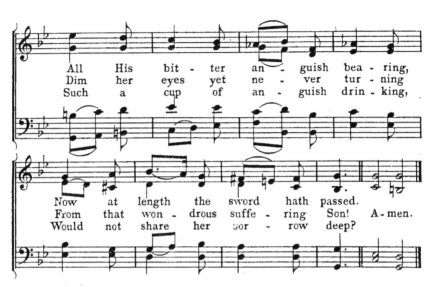

All His bit - ter an - guish bea - ring,
Dim her eyes yet ne - ver tur - ning
Such a cup of an - guish drin - king,

Now at length the sword hath passed.
From that won - drous suffe - ring Son! A - men.
Would not share her sor - row deep?

4. For His people's sins atoning,
   She saw Jesus writhing, groaning,
   'Neath the scourge wherewith He bled.
   Her beloved One, her Consoler,
   Saw she whelmed in direst dolor
   Till at length His spirit fled.

5. Fount of love and sacred sorrow,
   Mother, may my spirit borrow
   Somewhat of thy holy woe.
   May my heart, on fire within me
   With the love of Jesus, win me
   Grace to please Him here below.

6. Mother, every wound and tremor
   Of the Crucified Redeemer
   Firmly fasten in my soul.
   Every shame which thou art sharing
   O divide with me unsparing,
   Every pang and pain and dole.

7. Grant that I my tears may mingle
   With thine own in sorrow single
   For my Saviour Crucified.
   Let me, till my breath shall falter,
   Near to thee at Calvary's altar,
   Join my heart to Him Who died.

8. Queen of Virgins, best and dearest,
   Grant the prayer that now thou hearest:
   Let me ever mourn with thee.
   Let compassion me so fashion
   That thy Son's most sacred Passion
   Daily be renewed in me.

9. Be His Wounds my own transfixion,
   May His Blood of benediction
   Ebriate my soul entire.
   Virgin, when the mountains quiver,
   From that flame which burneth ever
   Shield me on the Day of Ire.

10. Christ, when I account must render,
    Be Thy Mother my defender,
    Be Thy Cross my victory.
    Dust to dust itself betaking,
    May my soul enraptured waking
    Paradisal glory see.

BLESSED VIRGIN MARY

Flos pudicitiae

1. Ma - ry mild, un - de - filed, Help of all the
2. Glo - ri - fied as the Bride, Ga - briel's A - ve
3. Shine a - far, Mor - ning Star, Christ the Sun - light

low - ly, O de - spise not our cries,
warns thee, And the Word, Christ the Lord,
lea - ding, Lend thine ear, Mo - ther dear,

Spring of hope most ho - ly.
For His birth a - dorns thee. A - men.
To our prayer and plea - ding.

4. Lift our eyes to the skies,
Raise our hearts, and bring them
Through thy might to the light
Of the heavenly kingdom.

Alma Redemptoris Mater

1. Mo - ther of Maj - es - ty, God's love a - dor-ning,
2. Born with-out stain of sin, Formed for the Ho - ly,

Thou that hast oped for man Hea-ven's high door,
Ga - bri - el's A - ve still Ri - ses to thee;

Star - of the O - cean-wave, Gate of the Mor-ning,
Vir - gin and Mo-ther pure, Ten - der and low-ly,

Look on our wan - de - rings, Thee we im - plore. A-men.
Hear us and plead for us Bowed at thy knee.

BLESSED VIRGIN MARY
Ave Regina coelorum

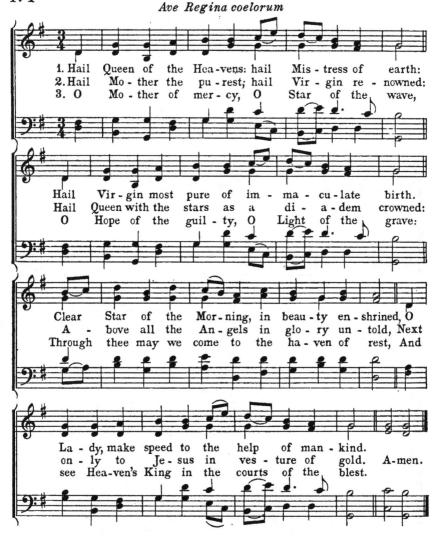

1. Hail Queen of the Hea-vens: hail Mis-tress of earth:
2. Hail Mo-ther the pu-rest; hail Vir-gin re-nowned:
3. O Mo-ther of mer-cy, O Star of the wave,

Hail Vir-gin most pure of im-ma-cu-late birth.
Hail Queen with the stars as a di-a-dem crowned:
O Hope of the guil-ty, O Light of the grave:

Clear Star of the Mor-ning, in beau-ty en-shrined, O
A - bove all the An-gels in glo-ry un-told, Next
Through thee may we come to the ha-ven of rest, And

La - dy, make speed to the help of man-kind.
on - ly to Je-sus in ves-ture of gold. A-men.
see Hea-ven's King in the courts of the blest.

4. These prayers and these praises I lay at thy feet,
O Virgin of virgins, O Mary most sweet.
Be thou my true Guide through this pilgrimage here,
And stand by my side when my death shall draw near.

1. Hail Queen of Heaven, the O - cean's Star To guide the
2. O gen - tle, chaste and spot - less Maid, We sin - ners
3. We dwel - lers in this vale of tears, To thee, blest

pil - grim here be - low; In tem - pest oft, we claim thy
make our prayers through thee: Re - mind thy Son that He has
Ad - vo - cate, do cry: As - suage our sor - rows, calm our

care, Save us from per - il and from woe. Mo - ther of Christ,
paid The price of our in - i - qui - ty. Vir - gin most pure,
fears And soothe with hope our mis - e - ry. Ref - uge in grief,

Star of the Sea, Pray for the wande - rer, pray for me.
Star of the Sea, Pray for the sin - ner, pray for me. Amen.
Star of the Sea, Pray for the mour - ner, pray for me.

4. And while to Him Who reigns above,
In Godhead One, in Persons Three,
The Source of life, of grace, of love,
We homage pay on bended knee,
Pray, O bright Queen, Star of the Sea,
Pray for thy children, pray for me.

BLESSED VIRGIN MARY
Salve Regina

1. Hail ho - ly Queen, Mo - ther of mer - cy sweet:
2. Born with-out stain, plead for our souls we pray;

Life of our souls, our hope, our ref - uge be.
Turn un - to us thy pit - ying eyes of love:

Chil - dren of Eve, ben - ding at thy dear feet,
So, while our lives pass from the earth a - way,

Out of the gloom, tear - ful we cry to thee.
Bring thou our souls safe to thy Son a - bove.

Chil - dren of Eve, ben - ding at thy dear feet,
So, while our lives pass from the earth a - way,

Out of the gloom, tear - ful we cry to thee.
Bring thou our souls safe to thy Son a - bove.

A-men.

BLESSED VIRGIN MARY

Regina angelorum

1. When - e'er I doubt if one so base as I
2. No ser - aph form, to hu - man weak - ness strange,
3. Mo - ther of God, Cre - a - tion's star-crowned Queen:

Shall share with heaven - ly choirs their joys se - rene,
Roy - al - ty's scep - tre holds in that high place,
Heaven's migh - tiest spi - rits bow be - fore thy feet,

This thought brings swee - test sol - ace to my soul,
But at the right hand of the King of kings
Yet 'mid the splen - dors of thy pomp di - vine

That thou, my Mo - ther, art the An - gels' Queen.
Thou sit - test throned, a daugh - ter of our race. A - men.
Our Mo - ther and our Sis - ter, too, we greet.

Tune reprinted by permission of the Missionary Society of St. Paul the Apostle of the State of New York. 4. Shall I then fear to face the glittering ranks
That guard the way to Heaven's most dazzling scene?
Their flame - tipped swords would lower at the cry:
'Angels of God, my Mother is your Queen.'

SAINT JOSEPH
Te Joseph celebrent

1. Jo - seph, pure Spouse of   that im - mor-tal Bride
2. Thee, when a - mazed con - cern for thy be - trothed
3. Thine arms em - braced thy   Ma - ker new-ly born:

Who shines in   ev - er   vir - gin glo - ry bright,
Had filled thy righ - teous spi - rit with dis - may,
With Him to   E - gypt's   des - ert didst thou flee:

Through all the Chris - tian climes thy praise be sung,
An   An - gel vis - it - ed, and with blest words
Him in Je - ru - sa - lem didst seek and find.

Through   all   the   realms   of   light.   A - men.
Scat - tered thy fears   a -   way.
O   grief, O   joy,   for   thee!

Tune
from

4. Not until after death their blissful crown
   Others obtain; but unto thee was given,
   In thine own lifetime to enjoy thy God
   As do the blest in Heaven.

5. Grant us, great Trinity, for Joseph's sake,
   Unto the starry mansions to attain,
   There with glad tongues Thy praise to celebrate
   In one eternal strain.

Arundel Hymns
by permission.

SAINT JOSEPH

Coelitum Joseph decus atque nostrae

1. Jo - seph, our cer - tain hope be - low,
2. Thee as Sal - va - tion's Mi - ni - ster
3. Joy - ful thou saw - est Him new - born

Glo - ry of earth and Heaven, Thou Pil - lar of the
The migh - ty Ma - ker chose, As Fo - ster - fa - ther
Of Whom the pro - phets · sang, Him in a man - ger

world, to thee Be praise im - mor - tal given.
of the Word, As Ma - ry's spot - less Spouse. A - men.
didst a - dore From Whom cre - a - tion sprang.

4. The Lord of lords and King of kings,
   Ruler of sky and sea,
   Whom Heaven and earth and hell obey,
   Was subject unto thee.

5. Praise to the Three in One Who thee
   Surpassing honors lend,
   And may thy merits be our aid
   To joys that never end.

1. Hail, ho - ly Jo - seph, hail, Chaste
2. Hail, ho - ly Jo - seph, hail, God's
3. Hail, ho - ly Jo - seph, hail, Prince

Spouse of Ma - ry, hail: Pure as the li - ly
choice wert thou a - lone, To thee the Word made
of the House of God; May His best gra - ces

flower In E - den's peace - ful vale.
Flesh Was sub - ject as a Son. A - men.
be By thy dear hands be - stowed.

Tune from Catholic Church Hymnal by permission of J. Fischer & Bro.

4. Hail, holy Joseph, hail,
   Comrade of Angels, hail:
   Cheer thou the hearts that faint
   And guide the steps that fail.

5. Hail, holy Joseph, hail,
   Father of Christ esteemed:
   Father be thou to those
   Thy Foster - Son redeemed.

SAINT JOSEPH

178

1. Great Saint Jo-seph, son of Da-vid, Fo-ster-fa-ther of our Lord,
2. Three long days, in grief, in an-guish, With His Mo-ther sweet and mild,
3. Clasped in Je-sus' arms and Ma-ry's, When death gen-tly came at last,

Spouse of Ma-ry ev-er-Vir-gin, Kee-ping o'er them watch and ward:
Ma-ry Vir-gin, didst thou wan-der, See-king the be - lo-ved Child.
Thy pure spi-rit, sweet-ly sigh-ing, From its earth-ly dwel-ling passed.

In the sta-ble thou didst guard them With a fa-ther's lo-ving care;
In the tem-ple thou didst find Him: O what joy then filled thy heart!
Dear Saint Jo-seph, by that pas - sing, May our death be like to thine,

Thou by God's command didst save them From the cru-el He-rod's snare.
In thy sor-rows, in thy glad-ness, Grant us, Jo-seph, to have part. A-men.
And with Je - sus, Ma - ry, Jo-seph, May our souls for ev-er shine.

1. Hail bright Arch-an-gel, Prince of Heaven, Spi-rit di-
2. Thine the first wor-ship was when gloom Through win-nowed
3. Thy zeal, with ho-liest awe in-spired, All o-ther

vine-ly strong, To whose rare mer-it hath been
ranks did move, Thus giv-ing God the sa-cred
zeals out-ran, With love of Ma-ry's hon-or

given To head th' An-gel-ic throng. A-men.
bloom Of young cre-a-tion's love.
fired, And of the Word made Man.

.For God to thee, O vision glad,
The Virgin-Mother showed,
And in His lower nature clad,
Th' Eternal Word of God.

5. Praise to the Three Whose love designed
Thee, champion of the Lord,
Who first conceived thee in His mind
And made thee with His word.

Christe sanctorum decus angelorum

1. Je - sus the Glo - ry of the Ho - ly An-gels, ThouWho hast
2. Let Thy Ar - chan-gel Mi - chael be our suc-cor; Peace-ma-ker
3. Send Thy Ar - chan-gel Ga - bri - el the migh-ty; Her - ald of

made us, ThouWho o'er us ru - lest, Grant of Thy mer-cy un-to us Thy
bles-sed, may he ba-nish from us Striving and ha-tred, so that for the
Hea-ven, may he from us mor-tals Spurn the old ser-pent, watching o'er the

ser - vants Steps up to Hea-ven, Steps up to Hea-ven.
peace-ful All things may pro-sper, All things may pros-per. A-men.
tem-ples Where Thou art worshipped, Where Thou art worshipped.

4. Send Thy Archangel Raphael, restorer
Of the misguided ways of men who wander,
Who at Thy bidding strengthens soul and body
With Thine anointing.

5. May the blest Mother of our God and Saviour,
May the assembly of the Saints in glory,
May the celestial Companies of Angels
Ever assist us.

6. Father Almighty, Son and Holy Spirit,
God ever blessed, Thou be our preserver;
Thine is the glory which the Angels worship,
Veiling their faces.

ANGEL GUARDIAN

181

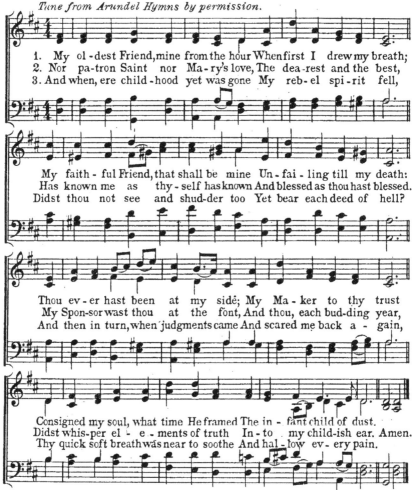

Tune from Arundel Hymns by permission.

1. My ol-dest Friend, mine from the hour When first I drew my breath;
2. Nor pa-tron Saint nor Ma-ry's love, The dea-rest and the best,
3. And when, ere child-hood yet was gone My reb-el spi-rit fell,

My faith-ful Friend, that shall be mine Un-fai-ling till my death:
Has known me as thy-self has known And blessed as thou hast blessed.
Didst thou not see and shud-der too Yet bear each deed of hell?

Thou ev-er hast been at my side; My Ma-ker to thy trust
My Spon-sor wast thou at the font, And thou, each bud-ding year,
And then in turn, when judgments came And scared me back a-gain,

Consigned my soul, what time He framed The in-fant child of dust.
Didst whis-per el-e-ments of truth In-to my child-ish ear. Amen.
Thy quick soft breath was near to soothe And hal-low ev-ery pain.

4. O who of all thy toils and cares
Can tell the tale complete,
To place me under Mary's smile
And Peter's royal feet?
And thou wilt hang about my bed
When life is ebbing low,
Of doubt, impatience, and of gloom,
The jealous sleepless foe.

5. Mine when I stand before the Judge,
And mine if spared to stay
Within the holy furnace till
My sin is burned away;
And mine, O Brother of my Soul,
When my release shall come:
Thy gentle arms shall lift me then,
Thy wings shall waft me home.

ANGEL GUARDIAN

Angelice patrone

1. My An-gel and De - fen.- der, In love I call to thee,
2. O Mas-ter kind and Com-rade, Di - rect my wave-ring will,
3. When I am sad bring com-fort, When weak thy power dis.- play,

The Guide and gen-tle Tea - cher That Heaven has sent to me.
Be near me as. my Lea - der, Be my De-fen-der still,
In thy dear arms up - bear me A - cross each rug-ged way.

Thanks for thy lov-ing kind.-ness My soul de-sires to give;
And keep me in the path.-way That leads to fields a - bove;
Let not my foot-steps fal - ter A - long the road of right,

Tune from Westminster Hymnal

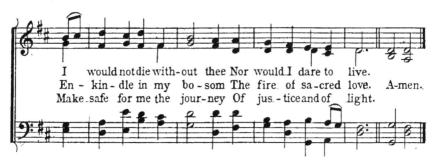

I would not die with-out thee Nor would I dare to live.
En - kin - dle in my bo - som The fire of sa - cred love. A-men.
Make safe for me the jour-ney Of jus - tice and of light.

4. My Comrade thou since childhood,
   In truth and love sincere,
   O fail me not, sweet Angel,
   When death's dark hour is near.
   Then aid my will to conquer
   The malice of the foe;
   What most to God is pleasing
   To my faint spirit show.

5. And in my final struggle
   A true contrition bring,
   That after pure confession
   No stains of earth may cling.
   In piety and patience,
   In faith and hope and love,
   So I may leave the regions
   Of earth for life above.

6. And when my trembling spirit
   Before the Judge shall stand,
   Bring then thy aid, dear Angel,
   Be thou at my right hand.
   O loving Guide and Comrade,
   In all my wandering way,
   Be always near to lead me
   To Heaven's eternal day.

183   ANGEL GUARDIAN

1. Dear An - gel, ev - er at my side, How lov - ing must thou be! To leave thy home in Heaven to guard A sin - ful child like me.

2. Thy beau - ti - ful and shi - ning face I see not, though so near; The sweet - ness of thy soft low voice Too deaf am I to hear; A-men.

3. But when, dear Spi - rit, I kneel down Both morn and night to prayer, Some - thing there is with - in my heart Which tells me thou art there.

Tune from Arundel Hymns by permission.

4. Yes; when I pray thou prayest too;
   Thy prayer is all for me;
   But when I sleep thou sleepest not
   But watchest patiently.

5. How very lovely they must be
   Whom God has glorified!
   Yet one of them, O sweetest thought,
   Is ever at my side.

6. Then love me, love me, Angel dear,
   And I will love thee more,
   And help me when my soul is cast
   Upon th' eternal shore.

SAINTS PETER AND PAUL

Decora lux aeternitatis auream

 184

1. It is no earthly summer's ray That
2. The blessed Seer to whom was given The
3. Fathers of mighty Rome, whose word Shall

sheds this golden brightness round, To crown with heavenly
hearts of men to teach and school, And he that keeps the
pass the doom of life or death, By humble cross and

light the day The Princes of the Church were crowned;
Keys of Heaven For those on earth that own his rule. A-men.
bleeding sword Well have they won their laurel wreath.

4. O happy Rome, made holy now
   By those two Martyrs' glorious blood:
   Earth's best and fairest cities bow,
   By thy superior claims subdued.

5. For thou alone art worth them all;
   City of Martyrs, thou alone
   Canst cheer our pilgrim-hearts and call
   The Saviour's sheep to Peter's throne.

6. All honor, power and praise, be given
   To Him who reigns in bliss on high,
   For endless, endless years in Heaven,
   One only God in Trinity.

185   SAINT PETER
Petri laudes exsequamur

1. O sing the great A - pos - tle In memo - ry of the Rock,
2. O Pe - ter, light of doc - trine And torch of ho - ly love,
3. 'Twas thine to tread the wa - ters; And when a - bout to sink

The ba - sis of that fab - ric Which fears not tem-pests' shock.
The ve - ry type of fer - vor And wis - dom from a - bove;
Christ's hand of help sus - tained thee, Close on destruction's brink.

To our Cre - a - tor's glo - ry That fes - tal chant shall burst,
Type too of sad trans-gres - sion, The fruit of faith - less fears,
So, when our faith is sha - ken And tossed by storms of ill,

We praise the sec - ond Shep - herd To glo - ri - fy the First.
And, from thy lapse up - ris - en, Of pen - i - ten - tial tears. Amen.
May Christ, for ev - er pres - ent, Bid winds and waves be still.

4. Thou from the cross didst follow
   Thy Master to the skies,
   And O be thou our leader
   That we too there may rise.
   By our good Shepherd's merits,
   And by his saving prayer,
   Thy trespass - laden people,
   Eternal Shepherd, spare.

SAINT PAUL
Paule doctor egregie

1. From thee, il - lus-trious Tea - cher Paul, Sounds forth the
2. O may thy stir - ring peal a - wake Our hearts, be-
3. O bliss of Paul be - yond all thought: To Pa - ra-

Chur - ch's trum - pet - call, Through-out the world from pole to
dew and fer - tile make; And so the rain from Heaven dis-
dise, yet liv - ing, caught, He hears the Heaven-ly Mys-teries

pole, Like tem - pest's blast, like thun - der's roll.
til, The par - ched soul with grace to fill. A-men.
there Which mor - tal tongue may not de - clare.

4. The Word's good seed around he flings,
   And straight a mighty harvest springs,
   And fruits of holy deeds supply
   God's everlasting granary.

5. The lamp his holy lore displays
   Hath filled the world with glorious rays,
   And doubt and error are o'erthrown
   That truth may reign and reign alone.

6. So long as endless ages run,
   To God the Father laud be done;
   To God the Son our equal praise
   And God the Holy Ghost we raise.

Ut queant laxis

1. O kind-ly help us, Ho-ly John the Bap-tist, Stained lips to cha-sten, fettered tongues to loo-sen; So by thy chil-dren may thy deeds of won-der Meet-ly be chan-ted, Meet-ly be chan-ted

2. Lo, a swift her-ald, from the sky de-scen-ding, Bears to thy fa-ther promise of thy greatness, How he shall name thee, what thy fu-ture sto-ry, Du-ly re-vea-ling, Du-ly re-vea-ling. A-men.

3. Scarcely be-lie-ving message so tran-scen-dent, Him for a sea-son power of speech for-sa-keth, Till with thy birth-tide joy-ful-ly re-tur-neth Voice to the voice-less, Voice to the voice-less.

4. Thou, darkly cradled in thy home so peaceful,
Knewest thy Monarch biding in His chamber;
Whence the two parents, through their children's merits,
Mysteries uttered.

5. Testifies Jesus, of the sons of woman
Birth ne'er was holier than of His Precursor;
Hence was it given thee to baptize in Jordan
Christ the Redeemer.

6. His be the glory, power and salvation,
Who over all things reigneth in the highest,
Earth's mighty fabric ruling and directing,
Only and Trinal.

Ut queant laxis

1. The proph-ets sang in sa-cred lay The
2. The world shall ev-er sing thy worth; Great
3. Of crowns twice ten the An-gels weave For

bright-ness of the com-ing day; Thy soul the glo-ry
Saint, it knows no ho-lier birth Than thine whose hands the
o - ther Mar-tyrs; some re-ceive A dou-ble glo-ry,

saw and calm Pro - claimed the pres-ence of the Lamb.
wa-ter poured Up - on the fore-head of the Lord. A-men.
but to thee Three hun - dred shi-ning wreaths shall be.

Tune from Catholic Church Hymnal by permission of J. Fischer & Bro.

4. And through thy prayers the Lord shall bless
   And light our souls with holiness,
   Shall lift our heavy hearts and deign
   To wash away all worldly stain.

5. To God the Father glory be,
   The same, Lord Jesus, unto Thee,
   And to the Spirit equal store
   Of praise and honor evermore.

SAINT IGNATIUS LOYOLA
Patron of Maryland Missions

1. Daunt-less Ig - na - tius, whose gen - e - rous soul,
2. Lea - ving the war - fare of prin-ces, you laid
3. Soon to your side in the Ar - my of God

Ear - ly am - bi - tious, made glo - ry its goal,
Proud-ly your sword at the shrine of the Maid.
Ral - lied com - pan - ions and for - ward you trod,

O with what cou - rage you con - quered your pride,
Ma - ry ac - cep - ted your chiv - al - rous sign:
Glad in the sor - rows of Je - sus to share,

Set - ting the world's emp-ty hon - ors a - side!
You would fight on - ly in war - fare di - vine. A-men.
Proud of the cross which His fol - low - ers bear.

4. Tender as Christ to the wayward and weak,
Stern when 'twas needful in anger to speak,
Like a true soldier, as gentle as brave,
This was your conquest, to strengthen and save.

5. Knight of our Lady courageous and true,
Lead us to battle, we'll march under you.
Noble Ignatius, your comrades, we'll go
Fearlessly forward to conquer the foe.

Aeterna Christi munera

1. Th' e - ter - nal gifts of Christ the King, Th' A-
2. The Church in these her Prin - ces boasts, These
3. In these the Fa - ther's glo - ry shone, In

pos - tles' glo - ry let us sing, And, while due
vic - tor - chiefs of war - rior hosts, The sol - diers
these the will of God the Son, In these ex -

hymns of praise we pay, Our thank - ful hearts cast
of the heaven - ly hall, The lights that rose on
ults the Ho - ly Ghost, Through these re - joice the

grief a - way. *(In Paschal Time)*
earth for all. Al - le - lu - ia. A - men.
Heaven - ly Host.

4. Redeemer, hear us of Thy love,
   That with this glorious band above,
   In heavenly bliss, through bounteous grace,
   Thy servants also may have place.

5. All laud to God the Father be,
   All praise, Eternal Son, to Thee;
   All glory ever, as is meet,
   To God the Holy Paraclete.

191 EVANGELISTS

Sinae sub alto vertice

1. From Si - nai's trem - bling peak, In trum-pet blasts from heaven And thun-ders of a threate-ning God, The ol - den law was given.

2. To us the self - same Lord, At - tem-pered to our gaze By veil of hu - man flesh, Him - self In love and grace dis - plays. A-men.

3. On gran - ite rock en - graved, The law from Si - nai's hill Pre - cepts sup - plied, but gave no strength Those pre-cepts to ful - fil.

Tune reprinted by permission of the Missionary Society of St. Paul the Apostle of the State of New York.

4. Stamped in the heart, the law
Which Christ proclaimed anew,
With its commandment, also gives
The strength to will and do.

5. This law with faithful pen
Ye wrote, O Scribes of God,
Preached it by holiest word and deed
And sealed it with your blood.

6. O may that Spirit blest,
Who touched your lips with fire,
Those same eternal Words of Life
Deep in our hearts inspire.

MARTYRS
Beate martyr prospera

192

1. Blest Mar - tyr, let thy tri - umph - day God's
2. Com - pan - ion now of An - gels bright, Thou
3. Be thou on this thy ho - ly - day Our

favo - ring grace to us con - vey; The day on
shi - nest clothed in robes of white; Robes thou hast
strong up - hol - der; while we pray That from our

which thy life - blood flowed And He thy crown in
washed in streams of blood, A daunt - less Mar - tyr
guilt we may be freed, Stand thou be - fore the

meed be - stowed. *(In Paschal Time)*
for thy God. Al - le - lu - ia. A - men.
throne and plead.

4. All laud to God the Father be,
And praise, Eternal Son, to Thee;
All glory ever, as is meet,
To God the Holy Paraclete.

193 CONFESSORS

Iste Confessor Domini colentes

1. This the Con-fes-sor of the Lord, whose tri-umph Now all the
2. Saint-ly and pru-dent, mod-est in de-mea-nor, Peace-ful and
3. Sick ones of old time to his tomb re - sor-ting, Sore - ly by

faith-ful cel - e-brate with glad - ness, This joy-ous feast-day
so - ber, chaste was he and low - ly, While that life's vig - or
ail-ments ma - ni-fold af - flic - ted, Oft - times have wel-comed

wears the wreath of hon - or In realms of glo - ry.
cour - sing through his mem-bers Quick-ened his be - ing. Amen.
health and strength re - turn-ing At his pe - ti - tion.

4. Whence we in chorus gladly do him honor,
   Chanting his praises with devout affection,
   That in his merits we may have a portion
   Now and forever.

5. His be the glory, power and salvation,
   Who over all things reigneth in the highest,
   Earth's mighty fabric ruling and directing,
   Only and Trinal.

VIRGINS

Jesu corona virginum

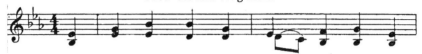

1. Je - sus the Vir - gins' Crown, do Thou Ac -
2. A - mongst the li - lies Thou dost feed, With
3. They, where - so - e'er Thy foot - steps bend, With

cept us when in prayer we bow; Born of that Vir - gin
Vir - gin Choirs ac - com - pa - nied, With glo - ry decked, the
hymns and prai - ses still at - tend; In bles - sed troops they

whom a - lone The Mo-ther and the Maid we own.
spot - less brides Whose bri-dal gifts Thy love pro - vides. A-men.
fol - low Thee, With dance and song and mel - o - dy.

4. We pray Thee therefore to bestow
Upon our senses here below
Thy grace, that so we may endure
From taint of all corruption pure.

5. All laud to God the Father be,
All praise, Eternal Son, to Thee;
All glory, as is ever meet,
To God the Holy Paraclete.

HOLY WOMEN

Fortem virili pectore

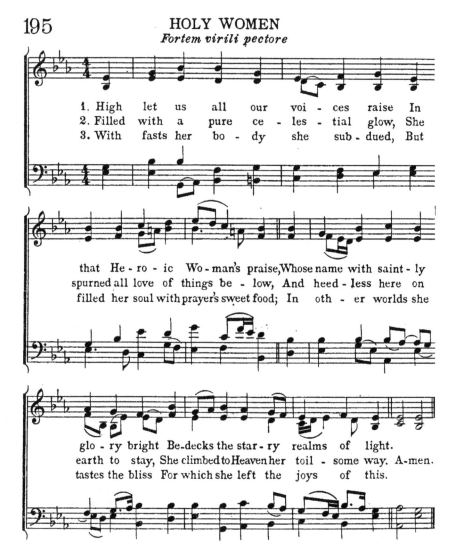

1. High let us all our voi - ces raise In
2. Filled with a pure ce - les - tial glow, She
3. With fasts her bo - dy she sub - dued, But

that He - ro - ic Wo - man's praise,Whose name with saint - ly
spurned all love of things be - low, And heed - less here on
filled her soul with prayer's sweet food; In oth - er worlds she

glo - ry bright Be-decks the star - ry realms of light.
earth to stay, She climbed to Heaven her toil - some way. A-men.
tastes the bliss For which she left the joys of this.

4. O Christ, the strength of all the strong,
To Whom our holiest deeds belong,
Through her prevailing prayers on high
In mercy hear Thy people's cry.

5. To God the Father, with the Son,
And Holy Spirit, Three in One,
Be glory while the ages flow,
From all above and all below.

ALL SAINTS

Placare Christe servulis

1. O Christ, Thy guil - ty peo - ple spare: Lo,
2. Ye An - gels hap - py ev - er - more, Who
3. Ye Proph - ets and A - pos - tles high, Be -

knee-ling at Thy gra-cious throne, The Vir - gin Mo - ther
in your cir-cles nine as - cend, As ye have guar ded
hold our pen - i - ten-tial tears, And plead for us when

pours her prayer, Im - plo-ring par-don for her own.
us be - fore, So still from harm our steps de - fend. A-men.
death is nigh, And our all-sear-ching Judge ap - pears.

4. Ye Martyrs all, a purple band,
   Confessors too, a white-robed train,
   O call us to our native land,
   From this our exile back again.

5. And ye, O Choirs of Virgins chaste,
   Receive us to the realm above,
   Where Hermits old from desert waste
   Unite to praise the God of love.

6. From Jesus' flock, O Spirits blest,
   Keep foe and faithless far away,
   That all within One Fold may rest
   Secure beneath One Shepherd's sway.

7. To God the Father glory be,
   And to His sole-begotten Son;
   And glory, Holy Ghost, to Thee,
   While everlasting ages run.

ALL SAINTS

Quisquis valet numerare

1. If there be that skills to rec - kon
2. Through the vale of lam - en - ta - tion
3. O what splen - dor, O what beau - ty!

All the num - ber of the Blest,
Hap - pi - ly and safe - ly past,
Ligh - tens round the hap - py place

He per - chance can weigh the glad - ness
Now the years of their af - flic - tion
From the King's dear roy - al Mo - ther,

Tune from Catholic Church Hymnal by permission of J. Fischer & Bro.

Of the ev - er - las - ting Rest,
In their memo - ry they re - cast,
From that ves - sel full of grace,

Which, their earth - ly war - fare fin - ished,
And the end of all per - fec - tion
While the le - gions of the Bles - sed

They by mer - it have pos - sessed.
They can con - tem - plate at last. A - men.
Gaze up - on her glo - rious face.

In her joy th' Angelic Cohorts
And the Saints that fill the skies
With the Apostolic Chorus
And the Martyrs sympathize,
While the Virgins and Confessors
Bend on her their loving eyes.

5. In a glass, through types and riddles,
Dwelling here we see alone,
Then serenely, purely, clearly,
We shall know as we are known,
Fixing our enlightened vision
On the glory of the Throne.

6. There the Trinity of Persons
Unbeclouded shall we see,
There the Unity of Essence
Perfectly revealed shall be,
While we hail the Threefold Godhead
And the simple Unity.

(197- 2)

ALL SAINTS

Supernae matris gaudia

1. Joy and tri - umph ev - er - las - ting
2. Here the world's per - pe - tual war - fare
3. There the bo - dy hath no tor - ment,

Hath the Heaven - ly Church on high;
Holds from Heaven the soul a - part;
There the mind is free from care,

For that pure im - mor - tal glad - ness
Le - gioned foes in shado - wy ter - ror
There is eve - ry voice re - joi - cing,

All our feast - days long and sigh:
Vex the qui - et of the heart.
Eve - ry heart is lov - ing there.

Yet in death's dark des - ert wild
O how hap - py that es - tate
An - gels in that ci - ty dwell,

Doth the Mo - ther aid her child;
Where de - light doth not a - bate!
Them their King de - light - eth well,

Guards ce - les - tial thence at - tend us,
For that home the spi - rit year - neth,
Still they joy and wea - ry nev - er,

Stand in com - bat to de - fend us.
Where none lan - gui - sheth nor mour - neth. A - men.
More and more de - si - ring ev - er.

4. There the Seers and Fathers holy,
   There the Prophets glorified,
   All their doubts and darkness ended,
   In the Light of light abide.
   There the Saints, whose memories old
   We in faithful hymns uphold,
   Have forgot their bitter story
   In the joy of Jesus' glory.

5. There, from lowliness exalted,
   Dwelleth Mary, Queen of grace,
   Ever with her presence pleading
   'Gainst the sin of Adam's race.
   To that glory of the Blest,
   By their prayers and faith confessed,
   Us also, when death hath freed us,
   Christ of His good mercy lead us.

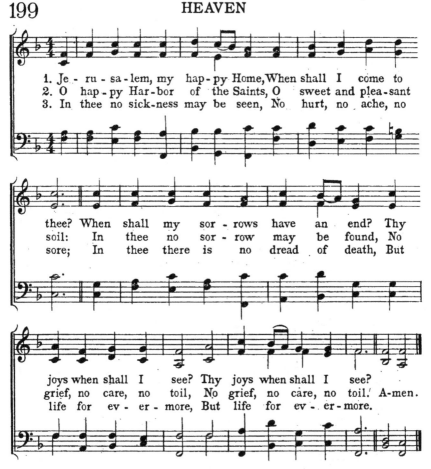

1. Je - ru - sa - lem, my hap - py Home, When shall I come to
2. O hap - py Har - bor of the Saints, O sweet and plea - sant
3. In thee no sick-ness may be seen, No hurt, no ache, no

thee? When shall my sor - rows have an end? Thy
soil: In thee no sor - row may be found, No
sore; In thee there is no dread of death, But

joys when shall I see? Thy joys when shall I see?
grief, no care, no toil, No grief, no care, no toil. A-men.
life for ev - er - more, But life for ev - er - more.

4. No dampish mist is seen in thee,
No cold nor darksome night;
There every soul shines like the sun,
There God himself gives light.

5. There lust and lucre cannot dwell,
There envy bears no sway,
There is no hunger, heat nor cold,
But pleasure every way.

6. Jerusalem, Jerusalem,
God grant I once may see
Thy endless joys, and of the same
Partaker ay to be.

1. Je - ru - sa - lem the Gol - den, With milk and ho - ney blest,
2. They stand, those Halls of Si - on, All ju - bi - lant with song,
3. The Throne is there of Da - vid, And there, from care re - leased,

Be - neath thy con-tem - pla - tion Sink heart and voice op - prest.
And bright with many an An - gel And all the mar - tyr throng.
The song of them that tri - umph, The shout of them that feast.

I know not, O I know not What joys a - wait us there,
The Prince is ev - er in them, The day-light is se - rene,
And they who, with their Lea - der, Have con-quered in the fight,

What ra - dian - cy of glo - ry, What bliss be-yond com - pare.
The pas-tures of the Bles-sed Are decked in glo - rious sheen. A-men.
For ev - er and for ev - er Are clad in robes of white.

Tune from Arundel 4. O sweet and blessed Country, *Hymns by permission.*
The home of God's elect:
O sweet and blessed Country,
That eager hearts expect.
O Christ, in mercy bring us
To that dear land of rest,
Who art with God the Father
And Spirit ever blest.

HEAVEN
Jerusalem luminosa

1. Light's A-bode, ce - les-tial Sa-lem, Vis-ion whence
2. Thou with beau-teous stones and pol-ished Won-drous-ly
3. There for ev - er and for ev-er Al - le - lu -

true peace doth spring, Brigh-ter than the heart can fan - cy,
art raised on high, Thou with pre-cious gems and crys-tal
ia is out-poured, For un - en - ding, for un - bro - ken

Man-sion of the high-est King; O how glo - rious are
Dec-o - ra - ted glo-rious - ly, And with pearls thy por-
Is the feast-day of the Lord. All is pure and all

the prai - ses Which of thee the proph - ets sing!
tals glit - ter, And with gold thy high - ways vie. A-men.
is ho - ly That with - in thy walls is stored.

Jerusalem luminosa, Pars II

4. There no cloud nor pas - sing va - por Ev - er damps or
5. There the ev - er - las - ting springtide Sheds its dew - y
6. What - so - ev - er trills of glad - ness From the song-bird's

shades the air; End - less noon - day, glo - rious noon-day
green re - pose, There the sum - mer in its glo - ry
swee - test throat, What - so - e'er de - li - cious con - cord

From the Sun of suns, is there; There no night brings
Cloud - less and e - ter - nal glows, For that Coun - try
Drops from mu - sic's tende-rest note, Strains a thou - sand

rest from la - bor, There un-known are toil and care.
nev - er · know - eth Au-tumn's storms nor win - ter's snows.Amen.
times more love-ly Round the Heaven-ly Ci - ty float.

203

HEAVEN
Jerusalem luminosa, Pars III

7. Youth with all its fresh - est vig - or
8. O how glo - rious, how re - splen - dent,
9. Now with glad - ness, now with cou - rage,

In - to age there can - not wane;
Frag - ile bo - dy, shalt thou be!
Bear the bur - den on thee laid,

There the old shall nev - er sor - row
When en - dued with so much beau - ty,
That here - af - ter these thy la - bors

For de - par - ted years a - gain:
Full of health and strong and free;
May with end - less gifts be paid,

No - thing past and no - thing fu - ture,
Full of vig - or, full of plea - sure
And in ev - er - las - ting glo - ry

Time doth pres - ent still re - main.
That shall last e - ter - nal - ly. A - men.
Thou with joy mayst stand ar - rayed.

10. Laud and honor to the Father,
Laud and honor to the Son,
Laud and honor to the Spirit,
Ever Three and ever One,
Consubstantial, Co - eternal,
While unending ages run.

(203-2)

HEAVEN

O bona patria

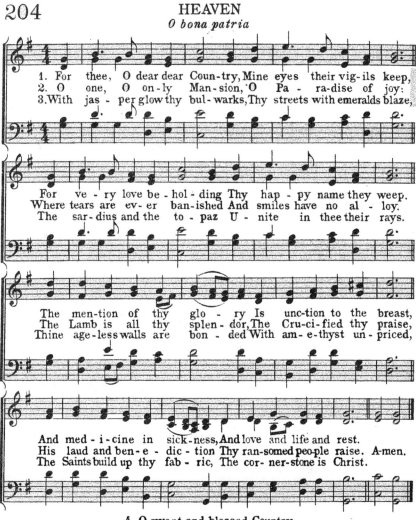

1. For thee, O dear dear Coun-try, Mine eyes their vig-ils keep,
2. O one, O on-ly Man-sion, O Pa-ra-dise of joy:
3. With jas-per glow thy bul-warks, Thy streets with emeralds blaze,

For ve-ry love be-hol-ding Thy hap-py name they weep.
Where tears are ev-er ban-ished And smiles have no al-loy.
The sar-dius and the to-paz U-nite in thee their rays.

The men-tion of thy glo-ry Is unc-tion to the breast,
The Lamb is all thy splen-dor, The Cru-ci-fied thy praise,
Thine age-less walls are bon-ded With am-e-thyst un-priced,

And med-i-cine in sick-ness, And love and life and rest.
His laud and ben-e-dic-tion Thy ran-somed peo-ple raise. A-men.
The Saints build up thy fab-ric, The cor-ner-stone is Christ.

4. O sweet and blessed Country,
The home of God's elect:
O sweet and blessed Country,
That eager hearts expect.
O Christ, in mercy bring us
To that dear Land of Rest,
Who art with God the Father
And Spirit ever blest.

In domo Patris

1. Our Fa - ther's Home e - ter - nal, O Christ,Thou dost pre - pare
2. A - midst the hap - py num-ber The Vir - gins' crown and Queen,
3. Th'A - po-stles reign in glo - ry, The Mar - tyrs joy in Thee,

With ma - ny di - vers man-sions, And each one pas - sing fair;
The ev - er-Vir-gin Mo - ther, Is first and fore-most seen,
The Vir - gins and Con - fes-sors Thy shi - ning brightness see;

They are the vic-tors' guer-don,Who through the hard-won fight
The Pa - tri-archs in tri-umph Thy prai - ses no - bly sing,
And eve - ry pa-tient suffe-rer,Who sor - row dared con-temn,

Have fol-lowed in Thy footsteps,And reign with Thee in light.
The Proph-ets of Thy wis-dom A - dore the na-tions' King. A-men.
For each es - pe-cial an-guish Hath one es - pe-cial gem.

4. The holy men and women,
 Their earthly struggle o'er,
 With joy put off the armor
 That they shall need no more;
 For these and all that battled
 Beneath their Monarch's eyes,
 The harder was the conflict
 The brighter is the prize.

5. And every faithful servant,
 Made perfect in Thy grace,
 Hath each his fitting station
 'Mid those that see Thy face.
 The bondsman and the noble,
 The peasant and the king,
 All gird one glorious Monarch
 In one eternal ring.

206

HEAVEN

Hic breve vivitur

1. Our life is here a brief one, Brief sor-row, short-lived care; The life that hath no en-ding, The tear-less life is there.

2. O hap-py ret-ri-bu-tion, Short toil, e-ter-nal rest; For mor-tals and for sin-ners A man-sion with the blest. A-men.

3. And mar-tyr-dom hath ro-ses Up-on that Heaven-ly Ground, And white and vir-gin li-lies For vir-gin-souls a-bound.

4. There grief is turned to pleasure,
Such pleasure as below
No human voice can utter,
No human heart can know.

5. We now must fight the battle,
But then shall wear the crown
Of full and everlasting
And passionless renown.

6. And now we watch and struggle,
And now we live in hope,
And Sion in her anguish
With Babylon must cope.

7. But He Whom now we trust in
Shall then be seen and known,
And they that know and see Him
Shall have Him for their own.

Paradisi gloria

1. O Pa - ra-dise, O Pa - ra-dise! Who doth not crave for rest? Who
2. O Pa - ra-dise, O Pa - ra-dise! The world is grow-ing old; Who
3. O Pa - ra-dise, O Pa - ra-dise! I great - ly long to see The

would not seek the hap - py land Where they that loved are blest?
would not be at rest and free Where love is, nev - er cold?
spe - cial place my dea-rest Lord In love pre - pares for me,

Where loy - al hearts and true Stand ev - er in the light, All

rap-ture through and through In God's most ho - ly sight. A-men.

Tune from Catholic Church Hymnal by permission of J. Fischer & Bro.

4. O Paradise, O Paradise!
   I feel 'twill not be long.
   E'en now I almost think I hear
   Faint fragments of thy song,
   Where loyal hearts.......

208

HEAVEN
Ad perennis vitae fontem

1. Who can sing in fit - ting num - bers
2. Winds of win - ter nev - er en - ter
3. Through the gree - ning fields and mea - dows

All the Joys of Heaven - ly Peace?
Those Su - per - nal Re - gions fair;
Streams of swee - test ho - ney flow;

There of liv - ing pearls are buil - ded
There the spring is ev - er - las - ting,
Mo - ving airs of spi - cy per - fumes,

Homes of ev - er - las - ting bliss,
Ro - ses bloom of ra - diance rare,
Soft a - ro - mas, breathe and blow;

Gol - den roofs and seats of glo - ry,
Flowers of eve - ry glow and o - dor
And in groves whose leaves are fade - less

Sweet with songs that nev - er cease.
Load with balm the lim - pid air. A - men.
Bloom and fruit to - geth - er grow.

4. There the moon and planets change not,
   Sun and stars no courses run;
   For the Light of that fair Country
   Is the Lamb, the Holy One,
   And His Day is ever shining,
   Ending ne'er as ne'er begun.

209 HEAVEN
Ad perennis vitae fontem, Pars II

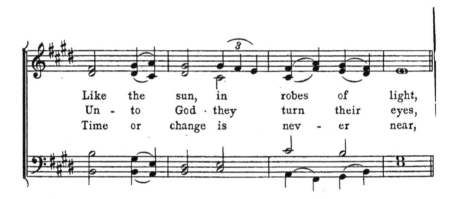

5. There the ho - ly souls are ves - tured
6. Lif - ted high o'er all mu - ta - tions,
7. True de - light lives on for ev - er,

Like the sun, in robes of light,
Un - to God they turn their eyes,
Time or change is nev - er near,

Crowned with daz - zling wreaths of tri - umph,
See the pres - ent Truth be - fore them
Nev - er mal - a - dy to tor - ture,

Glo - rious   vic - tors   in   the   fight,
Ev - er   shi - ning   in   the   skies,
Nev - er   age   to   blight   or   sear;

While   con - ju - bi - lant   their   prai - ses
And   they   draw   un - dy - ing   sweet-ness
Health   and   youth   and   ho - ly   plea - sure

Rise   un - to   the   God   of   might.
From   the   Fount   that   nev - er   dies.   A-men.
With   no   shade   of   chance   nor   fear.

HEAVEN
Ad perennis vitae fontem, Pars III

1. There is found the Ev - er - las - ting,
2. High in har - mo - ny those spi - rits
3. Gen - tle Je - sus, Crown of He - roes,

For the flight of time is flown;
Sound an end - less ju - bi - lee,
Guide me on Thy ra - diant way,

There is vig - or, health and beau - ty,
Praise in song the God of Bat - tles
Let me dwell in Thy fair Ci - ty,

For cor - rup - tion is un - known.
Through Whose mer - cy they are free,
See the glo - ry of Thy Day,

Death is dead a - mid the death - less,
Glo - ri - fy the King Tri - um - phant
March a com - rade in Thy Ar - my

All his power for ev - er gone.
Who hath wrought the Vic - to - ry. A - men.
In its ju - bi - lant ar - ray.

4. Fill my soul with strength and vigor
   For my warfare here below,
   Be Thy Name to me a bulwark
   In my struggle with the foe,
   And Thy sweet Reward hereafter,
   On my soul, dear Lord, bestow.

211   THE FAITHFUL DEPARTED
O vos fideles animae

1. Ye Souls of the Faith-ful, who sleep in the Lord,
2. O Fa - ther of Mer-cies, Thine an - ger with-hold;
3. O ten - der Re - dee - mer, their mis - e - ry see;

Who yet are shut out from your fi - nal re - ward:
These works of Thy hand in Thy mer - cy be - hold:
De - liv - er the Souls that were ran-somed by Thee:

O would I could lend you as - sis-tance to fly
Too oft from Thy path they have wan-dered a - side,
Be - hold how they love Thee de - spite of their pain:

From pris - on be - low to your pal - ace on high.
But Thee their Cre - a - tor they nev - er de - nied. Amen.
Re - store them, re - store them to fa - vor a - gain.

Tune from Rev.
of Hymns

4. O Spirit of Grace, Thou Consoler divine,
See how for Thy presence they longingly pine.
To lift, to enliven their sadness, descend
And fill them with peace and with joy in the end.

S. G. Ould's Book
by permission.

1. Lord, help the Souls which Thou hast made, The
2. Those Ho - ly Souls, they suf - fer on, Re -
3. For dai - ly falls, for par - doned crime, They

Souls to Thee so dear, In pris - on for the
signed in heart and will, Un - til Thy high be -
joy to un - der - go The sha - dow of Thy

debt un - paid Of sins com - mit - ted here.
hest is done And jus - tice has its fill. A-men.
Cross sub-lime, The rem - nant of Thy woe.

Tune from Arundel Hymns by permission.

4. O by their patience of delay,
Their hope amid their pain,
Their sacred zeal to burn away
Disfigurement and stain:

5. O by their fire of love, not less
In keenness than the flame,
O by their very helplessness,
O by Thy own great Name:

6. Good Jesus, help, sweet Jesus, aid
The Souls to Thee most dear,
In prison for the debt unpaid
Of sins committed here.

THE TRANSFIGURATION
Quicumque Christum quaeritis

1. All who de - sire with Christ to rise, To
2. Be - hold a Sun more old than night, A
3. Hail migh - ty King, Whose lov - ing sway The

Tha - bor's Mount lift up your eyes,
blaze of un - cre - a - ted Light,
Gen - tile and the Jew o - bey,

See there how Christ in glo - rious rays The
So high, so deep and vast of space, It
To A - bra'm prom - . ised, and de - creed, While

maj - es - ty of God dis - plays.
knows no bounds of time nor place. A - men.
earth shall last, to rule his seed.

Tune from Catholic Church Hymnal by permission of J. Fischer & Bro.

4. The law and prophets Thee unfold
And sign the truth by them foretold;
Thee God the Father from His throne
Commands the world to hear and own.

5. To Him be glory Who displays
To little ones His saving ways;
To God the Father we repeat
The same and to the Paraclete.

1. In days of old, on Si - nai, The Lord Al-migh-ty came
2. All hours and days in - clined there And did Thee wor-ship meet,
3. O ho - ly won-drous vis - ion, But what, when, this life past,

In maj - es - ty of ter - ror, In thun - der-cloud and flame.
The sun him-self a - dored Thee And bowed him at Thy feet,
The beau - ty of Mount Tha - bor Shall end in Heaven at last?

On Tha-bor, with the glo - ry Of sun-niest light for vest,
While Mo - ses and E - li - as, Up - on the ho - ly mount,
But what, when all the glo - ry Of un-cre - a - ted Light

The ex - cel-lence of beau - ty In Je - sus was expressed.
The co - e - ter - nal glo - ry Of Christ the Lord re-count. Amen.
Shall be the promised guer - don Of them that win the fight?

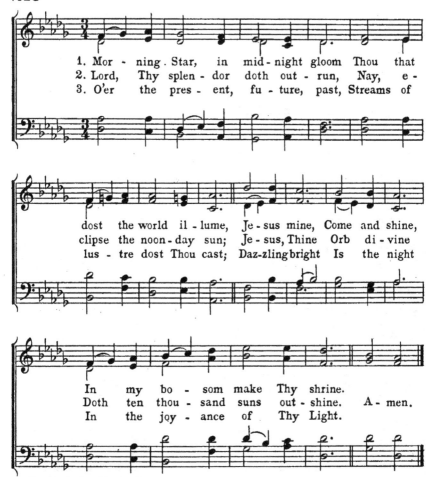

1. Mor - ning . Star, in mid - night gloom Thou that
2. Lord, Thy splen - dor doth out - run, Nay, e -
3. O'er the pres - ent, fu - ture, past, Streams of

dost the world il - lume, Je - sus mine, Come and shine,
clipse the noon - day sun; Je - sus, Thine Orb di - vine
lus - tre dost Thou cast; Daz - zling bright Is the night

In my bo - som make Thy shrine.
Doth ten thou - sand suns out - shine. A - men.
In the joy - ance of Thy Light.

4. To Thy beatific ray
   Everything doth worship pay;
   Star most clear,
   Far and near,
   Christ, Thy Godhead we revere.

5. Come then, golden Light, from far
   Speed the axles of Thy car;
   Jesus mine,
   Come and shine,
   In my bosom make Thy shrine.

1. Earth has no-thing sweet nor fair, Love - ly forms nor beau-ties rare,
2. When the day beams pierce the night, Oft I think on Je - sus' Light,
3. When I see in spring-tide gay Fields their va - ried tints dis-play,

But be - fore mine eyes they bring Christ, of beau - ty Source and Spring.
Think how bright that Light will be Shi-ning through e - ter - ni - ty.
Wakes the aw - ful thought in me, What must their Cre - a - tor be?

When the mor-ning paints the skies, When the gol-den sun-beams rise,
When as moonlight soft - ly steals, Heaven its thousand eyes re - veals,
Lord of all that's fair to see, Come re-veal Thy-self to me,

Then my Sa-viour's form I find Bright-ly im-aged on my mind.
Then I think Who made their light Is a thou-sand times more bright. Amen.
Let me mid Thy ra - diant Light See Thine unveiled glo-ries bright.

1. Praise to the Ho - liest in the hight,
2. O lov - ing Wis - dom of our God:
3. O wi - sest Love, that flesh and blood,

And in the depth be praise, In all His
When all was sin and shame, A se - cond
Which did in Ad - am fail, Should strive a -

works most won - der - ful, Most sure in all His ways.
Ad - am to the fight And to the res - cue came. Amen.
fresh a - gainst their foe, Should strive and should pre - vail.

Tune from Arundel Hymns by permission.

4. And that a higher gift than grace
   Should flesh and blood refine,
   God's Presence and His very Self
   And Essence all-divine.

5. O generous Love, that He Who smote
   In Man for man the foe,
   The double agony in Man
   For man should undergo.

6. And in the garden secretly,
   And on the Cross on high,
   Should teach His brethren and inspire
   To suffer and to die.

7. Praise to the Holiest in the hight,
   And in the depth be praise,
   In all His works most wonderful,
   Most sure in all His ways.

1. My God, how won-der-ful Thou art, Thy
2. How dread are Thine e-ter-nal years, O
3. How won-der-ful, how beau-ti-ful, The

Maj-es-ty how bright, How beau-ti-ful Thy
ev-er-las-ting Lord, By pros-trate spi-rits
sight of Thee must be, Thine end-less wis-dom,

mer-cy-seat, In depths of bur-ning light.
day and night In-ces-sant-ly a-dored. A-men.
bound-less power, And match-less pu-ri-ty.

Tune from Westminster Hymnal.

4. O how I fear Thee, Living God,
   With deepest, tenderest fears,
   And worship Thee with trembling hope
   And penitential tears.

5. No earthly father loves like Thee,
   No mother, e'er so mild,
   Forbears as Thou hast long forborne
   With me Thy sinful child.

6. Yet I may love Thee too, O Lord,
   Almighty as Thou art,
   For Thou hast stooped to ask of me
   The love of my poor heart.

7. Eternal Father, love's reward,
   What rapture will it be
   Before Thy throne prostrate to lie
   And gaze and gaze on Thee.

PRAISES OF JESUS

Laudetur Jesus Christus

1. When mor - ning gilds the skies My heart a - wa-king
2. O'er plain and hill and dell Peals forth the sweetchurch.
3. My tongue shall nev - er tire Of chan-ting in the

cries: May Je - sus Christ be praised, May Je - sus
bell: May Je - sus Christ be praised, May Je - sus
choir: May Je - sus Christ be praised, May Je - sus

Christ be praised. A - like at work and prayer To
Christ be praised. O hark to what it sings As
Christ be praised. This song of sa - cred joy It

Je - sus I re - pair. May Je-sus Christ be praised.
joy-ous - ly it rings: May Je-sus Christ be praised. A-men.
nev-er seems to cloy: May Je-sus Christ be praised.

4. To Thee my God above
   I cry with glowing love:
   May Jesus Christ be praised.
   The fairest graces spring
   In hearts that ever sing:
   May Jesus Christ be praised.

Laudetur Jesus Christus, Pars II

5. When first begins the day
O never fail to say:
May Jesus Christ be praised,
May Jesus Christ be praised.
And while at work rejoice
To sing with heart and voice:
May Jesus Christ be praised.

6. Be this at meals our grace
In every time and place:
May Jesus Christ be praised,
May Jesus Christ be praised.
Be this, when day is past,
Of all our thoughts the last:
May Jesus Christ be praised.

7. Does sadness fill the mind?
A solace here I find:
May Jesus Christ be praised,
May Jesus Christ be praised.
Or fades my earthly bliss?
My comfort still is this:
May Jesus Christ be praised.

8. Though break my heart in twain,
Still this shall be my strain:
May Jesus Christ be praised,
May Jesus Christ be praised.
The night becomes as day
When from the heart we say:
May Jesus Christ be praised.

Laudetur Jesus Christus, Pars III   221

9. In Heaven's eternal bliss
The loveliest strain is this:
May Jesus Christ be praised,
May Jesus Christ be praised.
The powers of darkness fear
When this sweet chant they hear:
May Jesus Christ be praised.

0. To God the Word on high
The Hosts of Angels cry:
May Jesus Christ be praised,
May Jesus Christ be praised.
Let mortals too upraise
Their voice in hymns of praise:
May Jesus Christ be praised.

11. Let earth's wide circle round
In joyful notes resound:
May Jesus Christ be praised,
May Jesus Christ be praised.
Let air and sea and sky
From depth to hight reply:
May Jesus Christ be praised.

12. Be this, while life is mine,
My canticle divine:
May Jesus Christ be praised,
May Jesus Christ be praised.
Be this th'eternal song
Through all the ages long:
May Jesus Christ be praised.

222   "FOR THOU ART WITH ME"

1. To win my heart with vis - ions bright and fair
2. Come, all ye proud ones of the earth, ar - ray
3. Death hath for me no fears; its bit - ter pains

Vain - ly the world with all its craft has tried;
Your gathe-ring hosts a - round me far and wide;
Shall nev - er from my King my heart di - vide.

Harm - less and weak its daz - zling wea - pons are;
My heart is calm a - mid the loud af - fray;
Faith - ful to death to Him my will re - mains;

I no-thing fear with Je - sus at my side,
I no-thing fear with Je - sus at my side,
I no-thing fear with Je - sus at my side,

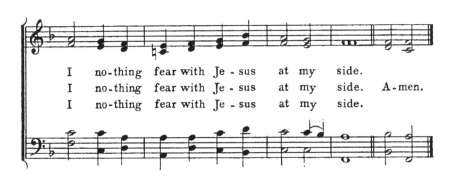

I no-thing fear with Je - sus at my side.
I no-thing fear with Je - sus at my side. A-men.
I no-thing fear with Je - sus at my side.

4. Though all the terrors of the last dread day
   With earth and hell together were allied,
   Though heaven and earth before me fled away,
   I nothing fear with Jesus at my side.

5. Jesus my Lord, my only hope and shield,
   No powers of ill before Thee can abide.
   My trust in Thee upon the battle-field;
   I nothing fear with Jesus at my side.

223
GOOD SHEPHERD
Dominus regit me

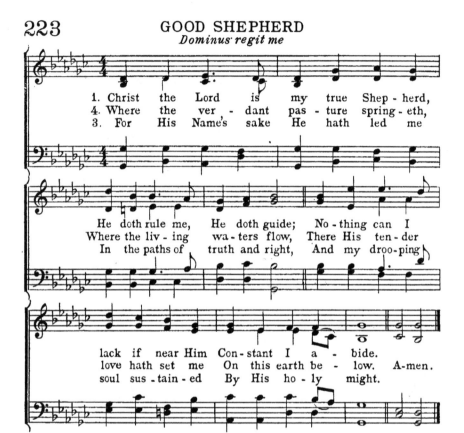

1. Christ the Lord is my true Shep - herd,
4. Where the ver - dant pas - ture spring - eth,
3. For His Name's sake He hath led me

He doth rule me, He doth guide; No - thing can I
Where the liv - ing wa - ters flow, There His ten - der
In the paths of truth and right, And my droo - ping

lack if near Him Con - stant I a - bide.
love hath set me On this earth be - low. A - men.
soul sus - tain - ed By His ho - ly might.

4. Though I walk through death's dark valley,
Yet no evil shall I fear;
Powers of darkness have no terrors;
Christ my Lord is near.

5. Where the wicked sore afflict me
He a table doth prepare,
Furnished well with food celestial
By His bounteous care.

6. He with oil my head anointeth
In the midst of all my foes,
And my cup with sweetness filleth
Till it overflows.

7. So throughout life's toilsome journey
Shall His mercy follow me,
Till at length in radiant glory
I my Lord shall see.

8. Bliss supreme, O bliss supernal,
Then to see Him and adore,
In His Heavenly House abiding
Blest for evermore.

*From
Catholic Hymns,*

*Cary & Co.
Publishers, London.*

Tune from Catholic Church Hymnal by permission of J. Fischer & Bro.

1. Faith of our Fa - thers, liv-ing still   In spite of dun-geon,.
2. Our Fa-thers chained in   pris-ons dark   Were still in heart and
3. Faith of our Fa - thers: Ma-ry's prayers Shall win our coun-try

fire and sword; O how our hearts beat high with joy
con-science free; How sweet would be their chil - dren's fate
un - to thee; And through the truth that comes from God

When-e'er we hear that glo-rious word! Faith of our Fa-thers,
If they like them could die for thee! Faith of our Fa-thers,
Our land shall then in - deed be free. Faith of our Fa-thers,

Ho-ly Faith: We will be true to thee till death. Faith of our Fa-thers,

Ho - ly Faith: We will be true to thee till death. A - men.

4. Faith of our Fathers: we will love
   Both friend and foe in all our strife,
   And preach thee too as love knows how
   By kindly words and virtuous life.
   Faith of our Fathers, Holy Faith:
   We will be true to thee till death.

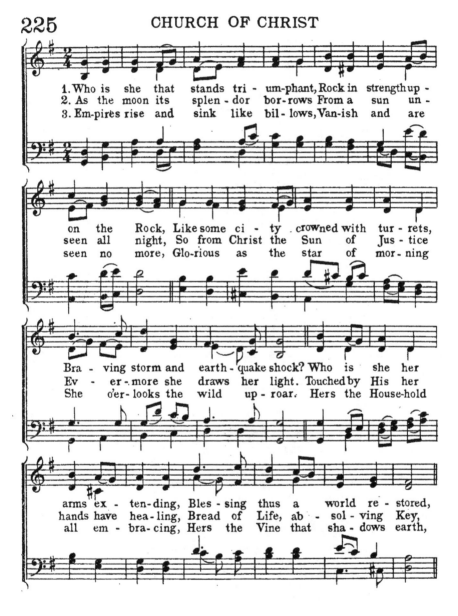

1. Who is she that stands tri - um-phant, Rock in strength up-
2. As the moon its splen - dor bor-rows From a sun un-
3. Em-pires rise and sink like bil - lows, Van-ish and are

on the Rock, Like some ci - ty crowned with tur - rets,
seen all night, So from Christ the Sun of Jus - tice
seen no more, Glo-rious as the star of mor - ning

Bra - ving storm and earth - quake shock? Who is she her
Ev - er - more she draws her light. Touched by His her
She o'er - looks the wild up - roar. Hers the House-hold

arms ex - ten-ding, Bles - sing thus a world re - stored,
hands have hea - ling, Bread of Life, ab - sol - ving Key,
all em - bra - cing, Hers the Vine that sha - dows earth,

All the an-thems of cre - a - tion Lif - ting to cre -
Christ In - car-nate is her Bride-groom, God is hers, His
Blest thy chil-dren, migh-ty Mo - ther, Safe the stran - ger

a - tion's Lord?
tem - ple she. } Hers the king - dom, hers the scep-tre,
at thy hearth.

Fall ye na - tions at her feet, Hers that Truth whose

fruit is Free-dom, Light her yoke, her bur - den sweet. A-men.

Tune from Arundel Hymns by permission.

1. Hail O New Je - ru - sa - lem, En-throned as a Bride, Rich with many a crim - son gem From 'Je - sus' pier - ced side. He that built thee on the rock In thee

2. Thou from one Bap - tis - mal Stream Re-ceiv'st thy ci - ti - zens; Thy sweet Pen - ance doth re - deem Poor bar - tered in - no - cence. Heat of strife or stain of clay Thou dost

3. Each new day's a - wake - ning fire Be-holds thy Ban - quet spread, Wine en - kind - ling fair de - sire And An - gels' Liv - ing Bread. Hence thy he - roes' faith - ful fight, Hence thy

folds and feeds His flock. He doth light and
cool or wash a - way In these sno - wy
maids' most high de - light; Fruit of plen - teous

li - ven thee By faith and hope and cha - ri -
tem - pered rills From God's e - ter - nal shi - ning
Cal - va - ry And seed of im - mor - tal - i -

ty, By liv - ing Faith and Cha - ri - ty.
hills, From His un - trod - den daz - zling hills. A-men.
ty, Of ev - er - las - ting joys to be.

From Arundel Hymns by permission.

4. When from all our fears and wars
   We wait the last release,
   May thy Unction smooth our scars
   And bring our senses peace.
   Then with honor lay us down
   And be mindful of thine own,
   Mother of our mortal way
   And of our spirit's endless day,
   Of Heaven's beatific Day.

VICAR OF CHRIST

1. Long live the Pope! his prai - ses sound A -
gain and yet a - gain; His rule is o - ver
space and time, His throne the hearts of men. All
hail the Shep-herd-King of Rome, The theme of lov - ing song,

2. Be - lea - guered by the foes of earth, Be -
set by hosts of hell, He guards the loy - al
flock of Christ, A watch - ful sen - ti - nel. And
yet a - mid the din and strife, The clash of mace and sword,

3. His sig - net is the Fish - er - man's, No
scep - tre does he bear, In meek and low - ly
maj - es - ty He rules from Pe - ter's Chair; And
yet from eve - ry tribe and tongue, From eve - ry clime and zone,

Let all the earth his glo - ry sing And
He bears a - lone the shep - herd - staff, This
Three hun - dred mil - lion voi - ces sing The

Heaven the strain pro - long. Let all the earth his
cham - pion of the Lord. He bears a - lone the
glo - ry of his throne. Three hun - dred mil - lion

glo - ry sing And Heaven the strain pro - long.
shep - herd - staff, This cham - pion of the Lord. A - men.
voi - ces sing The glo - ry of his throne.

From Catholic Church Hymnal by permission of J. Fischer & Bro.

4. Then raise the chant with heart and voice
In church and school and home,
Long live the Shepherd of the Flock,
Long live the Pope of Rome.
Almighty Father, bless his work,
Protect him in his ways,
Receive his prayers, fulfil his hopes
And grant him length of days.

Par-ce Do-mi - ne, par-ce po-pu - lo tu - o,

ne in ae-ter-num i - ra-sca - ris no - bis. Par-ce

Do-mi - ne, par-ce po-pu - lo tu - o, ne in ae-ter-num

i - ra-sca - ris no-bis. Par-ce Do-mi - ne, par-ce po-pu-

lo tu - o, ne in ae-ter-num i - ra-sca - ris no - bis.

Harmonies from Vincentian Cantuale

Cor Je - su sa - cra - tis - si - mum, mi - se - re -
re no - bis. Cor Je - su sa - cra - tis - si - mum,
mi - se - re - re no - bis. Cor Je - su sa -
cra - tis - si - mum, mi - se - re - re no - bis.

Harmonies from Vincentian Cantuale

EVENING

Jam sol recedit igneus

1. Be - hold the ra - diant sun de - parts In
2. By day, by night, our hymns of love We
3. All praise to Thee, blest Three in One, The

glo - ry from our sight, But, O our God, pos -
of - fer, Lord, to Thee; O may we sing with
God Whom we a - dore, As hath been paid in

sess our hearts With Thy ce - les - tial Light.
saints a - bove Thy praise e - ter - nal - ly. A-men.
a - ges gone And shall be ev - er - more.

Lucis Creator optime

1. E - ter - nal Source of Light's clear
2. The mor - ning and the eve - ning -
3. Re - move our past trans - gres - sion's

stream, Cre - a - tor of the sun,
tide A - like Thy gifts we hail;
load, From fu - ture ill pro - tect,

Who didst com - mand the day to beam, And
And Thou with us wilt still a - bide When
And in the straight and nar - row -road Our

straight - way it was done;
shades of night - pre - vail. A - men.
wande - ring feet di - rect.

4. So, knocking at the heavenly door
   And striving for the prize,
   We may above temptation soar
   And earthly joy despise.

5. These blessings of Thy love confer,
   O Father, with the Son
   And Holy Ghost the Comforter,
   Eternal Three in One.

232 EVENING

In manus tuas Domine

1. O Christ, Thou Bright - ness of the Day, That
2. We meek - ly pray Thee, ho - ly Lord, De -
3. O Mo - ther gra - cious, lov - ing, mild, Of

cha - sest night's dull shades a - way,
fend us through the night - ly hours;
mer - cy Mo - ther, un - de - filed,

Thou Splen - dor of Thy Fa - ther's Light That
Thou canst a ho - ly rest ac - cord; Grant
Drive back the foe, and to thy Son Con -

show'st His glo - ries to our sight.
that such ho - ly rest be ours. A - men.
duct our souls when life is done.

4. To Thee, O Jesus, Saviour sweet,
True Son of Mary, sinless Maid,
To Father and to Paraclete
All glory be for ever paid.

Fundere preces tempus est

1. 'Tis now the hour our prayers to pour, So warns the
2. The soul make clean, the mind se - rene, And work the
3. As one by one, when day is done, The sum - mer

day's ca - reer: 'Tis time to swell Thy can - ti -
work di - vine: In mer - cy weigh their prayers who
lights still glow, And o'er the face of eve their

cle Of praise, Re - dee - mer dear.
pray, And end - less life as - sign. A - men.
trace Of rud - dy ra - diance throw;

4. So when the pall of night shall fall
   Around us and above,
   With brightness cheer its mantle drear,
   And warm us with Thy love.

5. All praise to thee, O Father, be,
   In this our day's decline;
   Eternal Son, all holy One,
   Spirit, like praise be Thine.

EVENING
Te lucis ante terminum

1. As   now   the   day - light   dies   a - way,   By
2. Let   dreams   de - part   and   phan - toms   flee,   The
3. This   grace   on   Thy   re - deemed   con - fer,   O

all   Thy   grace   and   love,   Thee   Ma - ker   of   the
off - spring   of   the   night;   Keep   us   like   shrines   be -
Fa - ther,   with   the   Son   And   Ho - ly   Ghost   the

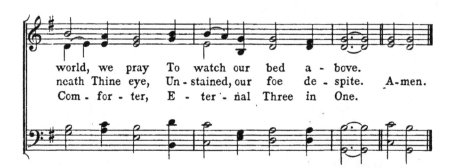

world, we pray   To   watch our   bed   a - bove.
neath Thine eye,   Un - stained, our   foe   de - spite.   A-men.
Com - for - ter,   E - ter - nal   Three   in   One.

1. O glad-some Light, O Grace Of God the Fa - ther's
2. Now ere day fa - deth quite We see the eve - ning
3. To Thee of right be - longs All praise of ho - ly

face, Th'e - ter - nal splen - dor wea - ring; Ce -
light, Our won - ted hymns out - pou - ring; Fa -
songs, O Son of God, Life - giv - er; Thee

les - tial, ho - ly, blest, Our Sa - viour Je - sus
ther of might un - known, Thee His In - car - nate
there - fore, O most High, The Heavens do glo - ri -

Christ, All joy in Thine ap - pea - ring.
Son, And Ho - ly Ghost a - do - ring. A - men.
fy And shall ex - alt for ev - er.

1. Sweet Sa-viour, bless us ere we go, In - to our minds Thy
2. The day is done, its hours have run, And Thou hast ta - ken
3. Grant us, dear Lord, from e - vil ways True ab - so - lu - tion

word   in - stil,   And make our luke-warm hearts to glow.
count   of all: The scan - ty tri - umphs grace hath won,
and   re - lease,   And bless us more than in past days

With low-ly love and fer - vent will.
The bro-ken vow, the fre - quent fall. Through life's long day
With pu - ri - ty and in - ward peace.

and death's dark night,   O gen-tle Je-sus, be our Light. A-men.

4. Do more than pardon: give us joy,
Sweet fear and sober liberty,
And loving hearts without alloy,
That only long to be like Thee.
Through life's long day. . . . .

5. For all we love, the poor, the sad,
The sinful, unto Thee we call:
O let Thy mercy make us glad;
Thou art our Jesus and our All.
Through life's long day. . . . . .

6. Sweet Saviour, bless us; night is come;
Mary and Joseph near us be;
Good Angels watch about our home;
And we are one day nearer Thee.
Through life's long day. . . . . . .

Number 39 should carry acknowledgment: *Tune from Arundel Hymns by permission*

Number 66, fifth verse, eighth line should read: *Who lives and loves and saves.*

Number 70, second verse, third line should read: *With eloquence their lips He strung.*

Number 73, first verse, fifth line should read: *With eloquence our lips inspire.*

Number 74 should carry acknowledgment: *Tune from Arundel Hymns by permission.* In third verse, second line should read: *O Solace Thou of all oppressed.*

Numbers 144 and 145, second verse, third line should read· *Blest be His compassion.*

ALPHABETIC
INDEX

INDEX

INDEX

No.	Translator	Remarks	Composer or Source of Tune
29	Monsignor Hall		J. Scheffler (?)
17			
123			*Plainsong*
100		*Abridged*	*Plainsong*
101		*Abridged*	C. Ballester, C.M.
70	E. Caswall		T. Arne
40	R. Campbell	*Abridged*	
55	J. M. Neale		J. Richardson
28	A. Riley		
13			*German*
213	T. J. Potter and others	*Adapted*	W. Ratcliffe
133	E. Caswall	*Adapted*	A. E. Tozer
57	E. Caswall, J. M. Neale and others		*Plainsong*
20			*French*
5	R. Campbell		*Anon.*
234	Cardinal Newman	*Adapted*	
51		*A cento*	*Plainsong*
168		*A cento*	*Italian: Adapted by* S. P. Waddington
58	R. Campbell		H. Carey
102			R. L. de Pearsall
103			
104			
230	R. Campbell		T. Tallis
36	E. Caswall		*German*
122			*Anon.*
124	H. T. Henry		G. H. Wells
125	H. T. Henry		A. Young, C.S.P.
192			*French*
3	R. Campbell		B. Millgrove
223			R. R. Terry
56	J. E. Leeson		*German*
90	G. R. Woodward		*German*
18	Canon Oakeley and others	*Adapted*	
68	E. Caswall		
72	E. Caswall		S. Webbe
229			*Plainsong*
41	F. C. Husenbeth		C. Stoecklin
7	E. Caswall	*Adapted*	*Plainsong*
66			R. R. Terry
189			
183			R. L. de Pearsall
142			R. A. Turton
216	F. E. Cox	*Abridged*	
231	R. Campbell		*Spanish: Harmonies by* G. R. Woodward
224		*Adapted*	H. G. Ganss
204	J. M. Neale		*German: Harmonies by* G. H. Palmer
191	E. Caswall		A. Young, C.S.P.

INDEX

INDEX

No.	Translator	Remarks	Composer or Source of Tune
186	. . . .	*Adapted*	*French*
15	Father Trappes.		
163	D. J. Donahoe	*Abridged*	*German*
144	E. Caswall	*Adapted*	J. Barnby
145	E. Caswall	*Adapted*	R. Filitz
178	Bishop Casartelli	. . . .	A. G. Stein
95	H. T. Henry and others	*A cento*	R. L. de Pearsall
179	. . . .	*Adapted*	S. Webbe
63	J. M. Neale	*Abridged and adapted*	O. Gibbons
177	. . . .	*Abridged*	H. Whitehead
173	D. J. Donahoe	. . . .	*Arranged from* O. Gibbons
147	H. N. Oxenham	*Abridged and adapted*	H. Whitehead
143	F. W. Faber	*Adapted*	V. Novello
152	. . . .	. . . .	R. R. Terry
226	. . . .	. . . .	S. Wesley
149	. . . .	. . . .	
150	. . . .	*Adapted*	H. L. Jenner
172	. . . .	*Adapted*	
171	E. Caswall	*Abridged and adapted*	*German*
84	R. Campbell	*Abridged*	*Plainsong*
69	R. Campbell	. . . .	
88	H. T. Henry	. . . .	
86	H. T. Henry	. . . .	*Italian*
87	H. T. Henry	. . . .	*Bohemian*
10	E. Caswall	*Adapted*	H. Whitehead
97	G. R. Woodward	*Adapted*	*French*
146	E. Caswall	*Adapted*	C. Gounod
195	E. Caswall	. . . .	*German*
79	C. A. Walworth.	. . . .	*German*
76	. . . .	. . . .	C. E. Miller
157	R. Campbell	*Adapted*	A. Young, C.S.P.
35	J. M. Neale	. . . .	
91	H. T. Henry and others	. . . .	*Plainsong*
92	H. T. Henry and others	. . . .	C. Ballester, C.M.
197	J. M. Neale	. . . .	A. E. Tozer
214	J. M. Neale	*Abridged*	*German*
221	E. Caswall	. . . .	*German*
78	H. N. Oxenham.	. . . .	Sir E. Elgar
54	. . . .	. . . .	*German*
184	F. W. Faber	. . . .	*German*
199	. . . .	*Abridged*	*German*
200	J. M. Neale	*Adapted*	R. L. de Pearsall
44	F. W. Faber	•	H. Isaak
99	. . . .	*Abridged*	R. R. Terry
140	H. W. Baker	•	*French*
34	R. Campbell	. . . .	J. B. Dykes
32	R. Campbell	. . . .	S. Webbe, jr.
180	. . . .	*Adapted*	*French*

INDEX

INDEX

No.	Translator	Remarks	Composer or Source of Tune
30	E. Caswall	. . . .	*German: Adapted by* J. Richardson
194	. . . .	. . . .	*German*
39	J. Austin.	. . . .	E. d'Evry
176	E. Caswall	. . . .	J. B. Dykes
175	E. Caswall	. . . .	*Italian*
198	. . . .	. . . .	*French*
123	. . . .	. . . .	*Plainsong*
80	E. Caswall	*Adapted*	A. Young, C.S.P.
19	D. J. Donahoe	. . . .	R. R. Terry
201	J. M. Neale	. . . .	*Plainsong*
129	. . . .	. . . .	H. S. Oakeley
227	. . . .	. . . .	H. G. Ganss
212	. . . .	*Adapted*	E. d'Evry
98	M. Russell, S.J.	*Adapted*	J. Langran: *specially arranged*
154	. . . .	. . . .	*French*
169	D. J. Donahoe	. . . .	*German*
1	R. Campbell	. . . .	S. Wehbe
215	G. R. Woodward	. . . .	*German*
170	D. J. Donahoe	. . . .	*German*
182	D. J. Donahoe	*Abridged*	R. L. de Pearsall
139	H. T. Henry	. . . .	*Anon.*
218	. . . .	*Adapted*	R. R. Terry
181	. . . .	*Abridged*	*German*
153	. . . .	*Abridged and adapted*	*Italian*
131	. . . .	*Adapted*	S. Wehbe
126	F. C. Husenbeth	*Adapted*	T. W. Staniforth
127	F. C. Husenbeth	*Adapted*	*German*
232	J. D. Aylward, O.P.	*Adapted*	T. Tallis
196	E. Caswall	*Adapted*	H. Whitehead
24	S. S. H.	. . . .	F. Westlake: *Arranged by* G. H. Wells
45	. . . .	*Abridged*	Monsignor Crookall
46	. . . .	*Abridged*	*Italian*
12	J. M. Neale	. . . .	*Plainsong*
134	H. T. Henry	. . . .	*Anon.*
81	. . . .	*Adapted*	Van Damne (?)
162	. . . .	*Abridged and adapted*	H. J. Gauntlett
151	. . . .	*Adapted*	*German*
235	. . . .	*Adapted*	Adam Drese
158	E. Caswall	*Adapted*	*French*
138	. . . .	*Abridged*	*Scottish*
137	M. Russell, S.J.	*Abridged and adapted*	S. Webbe
130	H. T. Henry	. . . .	J. Richardson
89	. . . .	. . . .	G. F. Bruce
31	J. D. Aylward, O.P.	. . . .	S. Webbe, jr.
33	E. Caswall	*Adapted*	T. W. Staniforth
187	. . . .	*Adapted*	*French*
65	W. J. Blew	*Adapted*	J. B. Dykes

INDEX

INDEX

No.	Translator	Remarks	Composer or Source of Tune
164	. . . .	*Adapted*	
207	. . . .	*Abridged and adapted*	R. A. Turton
14	J. O'Connor	. . . .	C. Barnekow
155	. . . .	*Adapted*	J. Groiss
156	. . . .	. . . .	*Arr. by* Nicholas Gatty
49	H. W. Baker	. . . .	Mozart
105	. . . .	. . . .	Werner
106	. . . .	. . . .	Duguet
107	. . . .	. . . .	A. E. Tozer
108	. . . .	. . . .	
109	. . . .	. . . .	*Plainsong*
110	. . . .	. . . .	A. S. Scott-Gatty
111	. . . .	. . . .	
112	. . . .	. . . .	R. L. de Pearsall
185	Mrs. Anstice (?)	. . . .	*German*
135	H. T. Henry	. . . .	*Anon.*
57	E. Caswall, J. M. Neale and others	. . . .	*Plainsong*
74	E. Caswall . . . . ' . .	. . . .	E. d'Evry
132	Rosa Mulholland	*Abridged*	*French*
77	E. Caswall	*Adapted*	S. Webbe
43	E. Caswall	*Adapted*	
47	E. Caswall	*Abridged and adapted*	R. R. Terry
23	J. M. Neale and others	. . . .	*Plainsong*
22	E. Caswall	*Adapted*	A. E. Tozer
85	E. Caswall	. . . .	J. E. Turner, O.S.B.
61	. . . .	. . . .	Mozart
205	J. M. Neale	*Abridged and adapted*	*French*
206	J. M. Neale and others	. . . .	*German*
113	. . . .	. . . .	*Plainsong*
228	. . . .	. . . .	*Plainsong*
217	. . . .	. . . .	A. Somervell
161	E. Vaughan	*Adapted*	
64	. . . .	*Adapted*	F. Giardini
27	. . . .	. . . .	
25	J. O'Connor	. . . .	
52	J. M. Neale and others	*Abridged*	J. E. Turner, O.S.B.
93	. . . .	*A cento*	
48	R. Campbell	. . . .	*German*
96	. . . .	. . . .	W. J. Maher, S.J.
73	E. Caswall	*Abridged and adapted*	*German*
75	E. Caswall	. . . .	*German*
2	R. Campbell	. . . .	*German*
50	. . . .	. . . .	*Plainsong*
167	. . . .	. . . .	*Italian: Adapted by* S. P. Waddington
159	E. Caswall	*Adapted*	R. Redhead
21	. . . .	. . . .	W. Birtchnell
11	J. M. Neale	. . . .	A. E. Tozer
8	Cardinal Newman and E. Caswall	*Adapted*	
236	. . . .	*Adapted*	G. Herbert

INDEX

INDEX

CPSIA information can be obtained
at www.ICGtesting.com
Printed in the USA
BVHW061213011218
534525BV00001B/76/P